A BETTER HIGH

A Humorous Look at Getting High Naturally, Everyday

Matt Bellace, Ph.D.

To Sarah, Zach + Andrew,

All the best!

Matt
Bellace

Inspired by the nationally renowned youth program,
"How to Get High Naturally"

ISBN: 978-0-615-32075-5

Attention Schools & Businesses:
This book is available at quantity discounts with bulk purchase for
educational, business, or sales promotional use.

For information, please contact Matt Bellace, PhD Presentations,
LLC at matt@mattbellace.com.

First Printing:
November 2009

WINTER OAK PRESS
Winter Oak Press is a division of Winter Oak Studios
Rockaway, New Jersey

Acknowledgements

To my wife, Dara, thank you for supporting me professionally and more importantly, personally, all of these years. You were supportive of me when I was a broke grad student in need of rent money and supportive of me when I asked you to edit this book despite being pregnant! To my son, Roy, who arrived the same week as this book and in half the time, you are our most precious gift. To Mom, Dad and my brother Mike, thank you for instilling in me the work ethic needed to complete this book and for inspiring so many good jokes.

To my TIGS friends, your laughter and enduring friendship is something that no amount of money could ever buy. To all the members and alumni of C.A.L.V.I.N. & H.O.B.B.E.S., thank you for making Bucknell University a better school to attend. To Bob Thomas, advisor to C.A.L.V.I.N. & H.O.B.B.E.S., thank you for supporting my interest in prevention since the age of 19. Thanks to my favorite Bucknell professor, Dr. Owen Floody, who inspired me to think critically and pursue further study in neuropsychology.

I want to say a special thanks to all of the audiences who ever laughed at my jokes and stories – without your laughs I would have never found the punch lines. Thank you to all the prevention advisors who have worked so hard to bring my message to your schools.

To my readers, I hope you will enjoy reading this book as much as I enjoyed writing it. I look forward to hearing your compliments…

Contents

CHAPTER ONE

How to Get High Naturally

"THIS WOMAN SAID TO ME, 'YOU DON'T DRINK?
WHAT A GREAT ACCOMPLISHMENT!'
I RESPONDED, 'I ALSO HAVE A PHD.'
SHE PAUSED AND SAID, 'YEAH, BUT NOT DRINKING...
HOW DO YOU DO IT?'"

-MATT BELLACE

The reconstructive knee surgery I had in 2007 taught me the difference between good pain and bad pain. When I woke up in the recovery room, my leg was in this machine that was bending it every thirty seconds. I was fine until the anesthesia wore off and I started making noises only dogs and mice could hear. My surgeon – Dr. Russell Warren – is the team doctor for the New York Giants and a man of few words. He watched me struggle on the machine and said, "You have to do this for the next six weeks, six hours a day, every day." I was devastated. Then he said, "But this is the good pain." I was thinking, "If that's the good pain, what's the bad pain? Punching me repeatedly in the groin?" Dr. Warren continued, "If you don't do this your knee will scar over and you might have a limp for the rest of your life." Then he looked at me and said, "But it is up to you," and left the room. I was thinking, "It's up to me? Pull the plug!"

When I was not at home on that machine, I was non-weight bearing on crutches for eight weeks. That experience taught me that snow and ice are not your friend. Also not your friend: tornados. I met a student in Kansas who survived a tornado while on crutches. I asked him, "Did people help you?" He said, "No. They just yelled, 'Get down!'" I also learned that people love to guess what happened to you. I often heard, "Was it skiing?" That is so rude especially if I don't even know you. Would you go up to a stroke patient in a wheelchair and ask, "Was it smoking?" No, that would be terrible. I am not ashamed to admit that there were moments during that time when I cried because it hurt so badly. But every time I wanted to pull the plug and quit, I realized that if I did I would be a hypocrite. How could I talk to students about good pain and then give up when facing it. Young people have it tough because they are faced with so many examples of good pain when they are young. It hurts to turn off a favorite television show and study for an exam. It hurts to stand up and be a leader at your school. It hurts to tell someone at a party, "I don't want to drink." I guarantee no young person will ever turn down a beer and then skip away singing a song. This is not High School Musical. You will never hear, "No thanks for the beer! We're all in this together…" These are examples of good pain because even though they hurt in the short term, some day young people will look back and be thankful for them. They will be thankful that they learned academic discipline, leadership or simple refusal skills. The good pain is also easier to get over.

The bad pain is reserved for people who choose to take the easy way out. They would rather cheat on a test than put in the work. They would rather complain about life than actually stand up and make a difference. They would rather have trust issues with their parents than tell their friends, "no." These are examples of young people choosing the bad pain. They qualify as bad pain because the negative consequences that come from them are not easily fixed. Failing out of college, an inability to be a leader in your life, and trust issues with parents are complicated to resolve. It is much easier to choose the good pain now over the bad pain later, but as Dr. Warren said, "It is up to you."

Prevention Speaking

"I don't like Dr. Phil because he comes on his show and tells his patients exactly what's wrong with them. Any good psychologist knows — you keep that a secret."
- Matt Bellace

I have been fortunate for over a decade to travel the country and speak with young people about making healthy choices. As you might expect, adolescents are usually thrilled when they hear there will be another assembly related to not doing drugs. The e-mails I receive from students after my programs often begin with, "When I heard there was going to be a drug speaker, I thought, 'This is going to suck. I'll just sleep through it.'" I was lucky to have learned from watching some of the great speakers and legendary comedians how to entertain while making a point. More importantly, I never say "Don't do drugs" because I know that won't stop young people from doing drugs. It will, however, stop them from listening to me. Instead I share laughs, some of my story, and insights from patients that I have treated. In the end, if students walk away from my program having heard me out then I win and so do they. Honestly, it is a victory that after so many years I don't live in a van down by the river.

Telling people how to live their life does not change behavior. If it did, psychotherapy could last one session and everyone would be cured. Real behavioral change takes empathy, guidance, and time. I usually only get an hour or so to have an impact on an audience, so I choose to focus on supporting positive choices. Psychologists believe it is easier to shape behavior by supporting a positive choice rather than punish a negative one. To accomplish my program goals, I structure the talk by presenting an acronym – L.E.A.D. I created the acronym because it helps the audience remember what I talked about, but I also believe that living a naturally high lifestyle requires being a leader in your own life. The four points of L.E.A.D. are: Leaning on healthy people for support, Expressing your emotions in a healthy way, Achieving natural highs every day, and Don't be afraid to take a stand.

Lean on Healthy People for Support

*"If my dad gets bored with your conversation, he will just get
up and leave the room.
That hurts when you're the only two people in the room."*
-Matt Bellace

I played football in high school, which if you knew me would be hard
to believe because I am built more like a reader. I was a quarterback
at Montclair High School (Montclair, NJ) three years before New
York Giants Super Bowl hero David Tyree started playing his high
school ball there. My fondest memory came in my senior year. It
was the fourth quarter of a tie game against Clifton High School.
There was one minute to go in the game when I threw that pass
all quarterbacks dream of throwing – the ball was intercepted and
returned seventy-five yards for a touchdown. We were losing by
seven points and our coach was so angry he benched me and put in
the backup quarterback for the final plays. With only a few seconds
left, our backup quarterback threw a fifty-yard desperation pass that
our receiver Darnell Williams caught and ran into the end zone as
time ran out on the clock. Our coach decided to go for the two-point
extra point to win the game instead of kicking for the tie. Amazingly,
he put me back in the game, but I later found out it was because the
other guy did not know the play. I remember being so nervous my
hands were shaking, which is not good when you get underneath
the wrong lineman. I got underneath the correct lineman, called
"Hike!," rolled out, and threw the ball in the direction of our best
player, Jason Curry. The pass was a beautiful tight spiral. Jason
reached out his hands and the ball sailed six inches away from his
fingertips. I put my head down in shame just as our fans erupted in
cheers. I looked up and realized that another wide receiver had seen
the ball was going to be overthrown – probably because he knew I
was throwing it – and made a diving catch in the back of the end
zone to win the game.

When I tell this story in schools sometimes I get that look that
says, "So, what happened next?" Well, a reporter from The Newark

Star Ledger newspaper came up to me in our locker room and said, "That was incredible! You rolled out and saw Jason was covered, looked him off and threw the ball right to the other guy. What do you have to say?" I leaned back in my chair and said, "Yup. That's pretty much how it happened, son." I don't know why we used words like "son" in my high school, but Montclair High is such a diverse school that you could walk down the hall and hear all kids of words, like "What's up, nephew?" To which I once responded, "That's not your nephew! Clearly that's a girl."

I selfishly tell the football story for a reason. I had two groups of friends in high school. The popular group of friends thought their unofficial job was to put down everyone and everything at the school. After the game, my popular friends said things like, "Ah, Bellace you got lucky. You shouldn't be playing quarterback. You suck." My second group of friends was much different. They were not as popular, but that did not seem to bother them. They were much more supportive. After the game they came up to me with nothing but high fives and hugs. It is almost twenty years later and I am still close with some of those supportive friends. We have been in each other's lives through the good times and the bad. I can honestly say that without their support I would not be who I am today. If you are wondering about the popular friends, well they are buried deep in my Facebook page, but I don't know them. I guess I never did.

Leaning on healthy people for support could be the most important part of living a naturally high lifestyle. If you are surrounded by positive support it can encourage you to step outside of your comfort zone and try new things. This is why the National Institute of Drug Abuse lists the number one protector against adolescent substance abuse as strong and positive social support. This support can be in the form of friends, family, religious or service organizations, teachers, or coaches. It is not who it is, but the quality of the support that matters. In my opinion, it is especially important to have a small group of fun, supportive friends you can rely upon. Let's face it – the right friends can even make waiting on line fun.

If you feel like your support is made up of some negative influences, I can sympathize. I grew up in an Italian family in

Northern New Jersey with a dad who looked like a smaller version of Tony Soprano. In some ways my family acted like the Sopranos, too. No one ever got decapitated, but I heard plenty of critical comments and negativity. When the stock market collapsed in the fall of 2008, someone asked me if my father – who worked on Wall Street for over 30 years – was upset. I said, "Upset? He is the most relaxed I have ever seen him. He has been waiting for this his entire life."

I am fortunate that despite any negativity in my family, they happen to be supportive. They have always been there for me when it mattered most. I am fortunate that they are healthy and that I get to spend time with them. However, telling jokes about my family is how I cope with their eccentricities. I developed this coping mechanism at an early age. The most difficult period of time for my family during my lifetime occurred while I was in middle school. I watched arguments on an almost nightly basis between my older brother and my parents. These arguments were centered on my brother and his poor adolescent choices. My brother is five years older than me and in high school he was very social. He hung out with the party-holic crowd. They were into drinking, drugs and other high risk behaviors. The fact that many young people his age were doing it was really not an excuse. What seemed to upset my parents most was that my brother would get caught doing something wrong and then defend his behavior rather than take responsibility for it. He would say things like, "Mom and Dad are just jealous. They wish they could have fun like me." Yeah, it was real Jerry Springer stuff.

The way I coped with all the arguments was to find humor in the pain. Fortunately for me there were a lot of funny moments. Like the day my brother decided he was going to be blonde. So he gets this spray called Sun-In – similar to bleach – poured it all over his black hair and went out into the sun. Two hours later his head looked like an orange highlighter. That happened to be the week my father decided to take the family picture. To this day, in my parents' living room there is a big picture of three Bellace's and Danny Bonnaducci.

In the beginning, I would go to my room when the yelling broke out. Eventually, I became so used it that I stayed for all the great material. One time my brother was being lectured on why beer was bad for teenagers and he responded, "Relax, I heard there's protein in beer."

My brother "failed out" of Lycoming College in Pennsylvania after his first semester. He probably could have returned, but my parents felt that he wasn't even trying. I find it ironic that all the partying and rebelling against my parents landed him in the one place you would think he would be horrified to end up – back home. It is also ironic that Lycoming College has hired me for the past five years to speak at their freshman orientation. When they first hired me they knew nothing about my brother's time there. Now I look forward to each year there.

I remember those days as some of the worst in my family's history and not just because of my bother's behavior. My maternal grandfather, Roy Basso (or "Pops" as we called him) passed away around the same time from pancreatic cancer. He was the mayor of Point Pleasant Beach, NJ, owner of an Oldsmobile dealership in town, and truly beloved by everyone who knew him. When he passed away there was a funeral procession that stretched over a mile long – a big deal in a town a mile long. There could have been one car at the funeral and it would never change the fact that Pops was the biggest role model in my young life. His death created a vacuum in our family that has never been filled.

As I look back, two positive things came out of my brother's turmoil. First, the bad pain of failing out of college and having to pay my parents back for his first semester's tuition eventually helped him focus and get his life back on track. To my knowledge, the biggest change my brother made during his second chance in college was to surround himself with more supportive people. He went to American International College and they had an excellent learning center, which helped get him through. I am very proud of my brother for putting his life together and moving in a positive direction. There are many examples of people who just give up after failing out of college, never to return. He never gave up and that is honorable.

The second best thing to come out of those days was my decision – in eighth grade – not to drink or do drugs. We live in such a crazy time that making the decision not to drink or do drugs could actually be the basis for a career. One night I announced at the dinner table, "I will never drink or do drugs." I imagined my mom would be so happy she would just hug me and say, "Son, you have no curfew. You can drive the car." I'd be like, "Mom, I'm only twelve." She would say, "It doesn't matter." For some reason, my real announcement did not impress her as much as I thought it would. In the summer of 1989, as a sophomore at Montclair High, my mother sent me to a leadership and prevention conference called the Teen Institute of the Garden State (T.I.G.S.). I guess she didn't send me as much as she made me go. It was the last week of summer vacation and I was so mad about it that I started making up lies to get out of it. I said, "Mom, I heard this conference is just for recovering alcoholics." My mom hated that one. When I arrived at the camp there were counselors on stage, in costumes, cheering and I said, "Look! They're still drinking!" It would not have mattered anyway, because my mom would have never let me leave. She was the vice principal at my high school and a tough woman. Guys would stop me in the hall and say, "I'm going to kill you. Your mom gave me two weeks detention." To which I would reply, "I'm not afraid of you. I live with her."

T.I.G.S. was marketed as a statewide prevention program which empowered students to be drug-free. For me, it went from feeling like a death sentence to a magical place almost over night. The camp was deep in the woods outside of Blairstown, NJ. Yes, New Jersey has deep woods. It featured ropes courses, great motivational speakers/ comedians, and small group discussions. I can still remember how empowering it felt to have an adult ask me for my opinion and actually listen non-judgmentally. The best part was making friends from other schools and of course, the four-to-one girl-to-guy ratio.

As I look back on it now, the conference did something very progressive. They did not use scare tactics to convince young people to behave. Scare tactics have been proven not to work when it comes to drug and alcohol prevention. A speaker can come into a school and tell kids, "Drugs and alcohol will kill you" (which they can). However, over the course of the year those students will go out to about a dozen parties, look around at their friends and think, "Guess what? None of us are dead!" The real problem is that drug and alcohol abuse does not kill people quickly enough. That is a pretty dark thing to say, but what do you think would happen if one teen died every time there was a drinking or drug party in your town? Well, first of all people would walk real slowly into those parties. They would be saying, "Who's it going to be tonight? Not it!" If drug and alcohol abuse killed one student at every party the problem with drugs and alcohol would practically disappear in this country. Psychology teaches us that punishing something quickly and consistently changes behavior. The problem with drug and alcohol abuse is that it can go on for years before the user feels the bad pain from his or her negative behaviors.

The T.I.G.S. conference somehow knew that scare tactics do not work. Instead, they focused on empowerment. They inspired us to achieve greatness in our lives. I am not sure everyone responded, but I did. I got the message: If you want to be better than you are today, you have to want to be healthy. I was all about internal motivation to do something positive. By the time the five days ended, I went from hating it to loving it. I went from dying to leave to dying to come back as one of those crazy costumed counselors.

I was rejected the first time I attempted to return to T.I.G.S as a counselor. It is ironic now, but it was devastating. The following year I matured quite a bit and re-applied. The second time I was accepted and went to have a great experience. In fact, it was during that counselor year that I bonded with all of those supportive friends that I still hold so dear. The responsibilities of the counselors at camp included putting on skits, role modeling healthy behavior, and genuinely helping others. If you were really lucky, you would be asked to speak in front of the camp. Dave Johnston, the leader of the counselors, saw something in me and made sure that I would speak to the group. It was probably less than five minutes, but the experience gave me my first taste of being a social activist. I created part of my identity at that conference. Yet, without the friends I met there, I would have had little chance to carry the behavior back home.

Exercise: Are you interested in attending a Teen Institute or high school prevention conference like it? There are almost a dozen active in the United States under the umbrella of the National Association of Teen Institutes (www.teeninstitute.org). New Jersey's Teen Institute has been through some unfortunate turmoil over the years, through no fault of its own. Today it is called the Lindsey Meyer Teen Institute (L.M.T.I.), named after an inspirational young woman who attended the program in the late 1990's (www.lmteeninstitute.org). There are also very similar and more popular programs around the country – such as Youth to Youth International (www.y2yint.com) and Students Against Destructive Decisions (www.sadd.org) – that also have great local and national conferences that do much the same as the one I attended in 1989.

Brain Facts: Environment
Reading science articles does not cause me to break out a highlighter much these days. I guess after 21 years of school I have done enough of that. However, the June 25, 2006 edition of the New York Times had me highlighting like an eighth grader again. In a great Science Times article called "An Anti-Addiction Pill," by Benoit Denizet-Lewis, there was a reference to a study called "Rat Park."[1] This was an elegant 1980's research study performed by Dr. Bruce Alexander from the Department of Psychology at Simon Fraser University (British Columbia, Canada).[2] The hypothesis was simple: Rats that lead stressful, boring lives would self-medicate (i.e., drink a sweet substance with a heroin-like drug in it) when given the chance, and rats with stimulating, lower stress lives would not self-medicate.

Dr. Alexander first constructed two very different rat environments. The low stress environment was called "Rat Park" and it had ample access to food and water, along with natural vegetation and rat toys. You know – rat I-Pods, rat Xboxes, etc. The high stress environment was much smaller, more isolating, and had no toys. The one similarity among the two environments was access to a sweet drink containing a heroin-like substance that the rats could drink when desired – rats love sweet drinks. After a week, they measured the amount of heroin-sweet drink consumed by the rats living in the two environments. The results were surprising, as the "Rat Park" animals were having too much fun to drink more than a little of the heroin drink, regardless of how sweet Dr. Alexander made it. The isolated and stressed rats, on the other hand, often got high, drinking more than a dozen times the amount of the morphine solution as the "Rat-Parkers." Other studies since have supported the notion that the environment can play a big role in the behavior of drug abuse.[3,4]

The Alexander study serves as an important reminder that genetic make up is not everything when it comes to addiction. A stimulating and supportive environment – especially during childhood and adolescence – is a strong protector against addiction. Addicts are more likely to have been unnecessarily stressed during childhood and they are less able to deal with stress as adults.[4] These stressors can include neglect, emotional, physical or sexual abuse, or poverty. Studies show that animals stressed during early development were more likely to self-administer drugs later in life.[3] In contrast, living in an enriched, lower stress environment appears to protect animals from developing addictive behaviors.[1] It is probably safe to assume the same process occurs for humans.

Express Your Emotions in a Healthy Way

> *"My wife and I are both psychologists,*
> *which means we have very short arguments.*
> *'Do you know how that makes me feel, Matt?'*
> *'Yes, I do. I'm afraid that is all the time we have left.'"*
> *-Matt Bellace*

I attended elementary school in a New Jersey town called Little Falls.

It was hard telling my friends where I was from because they would ask, "Do you live in Little Balls?" The elementary school in our town was called School Number Two, but the middle school was School Number One. I guess the school board naming committee had a real dislike for creativity and ascending numbers. One of my favorite things about elementary school was science class because I never knew what was going to happen. We had one girl who performed her own science experiment – she saved her sour milk cartons in her desk every day for a month. One day the kid next to her got a whiff of it and jumped out of his seat. He screamed, "Oh, that's gross!" But it was third grade so thirty seconds later the kid sat down, cupped his hand and sniffed it again. He screamed and then told me to smell it.

The day that changed my life was when our teacher Ms.Goya put a plant on each one of our desks and explained that we would have to take care of it. My plant was a spider plant and the year was 1983. Growing up in North Jersey I did not receive a lot of plants as gifts. If you grew up in Kansas, maybe when you hit third grade your parents gave you ten acres. I don't know. The concept of having a plant of my own was so foreign that it became a very special thing for me. By the end of the year, Ms. Goya gave us our plants to bring home. I was so excited that I began reading about plant biology and exploring the outside world. Today, over twenty five years later, I have three huge spider plants in my New York City apartment. On the wall a few feet away is my framed PhD degree in Clinical Psychology from Drexel University. I can honestly say that if it wasn't for that science class and encouragement from teachers and family, I never would have pursued the degree. Let's face it – there are not a lot of Italian Ph.D.'s. I think it is just me and Galileo.

Learning and sharing information with others is one of my favorite forms of self-expression. Spider plants are amazing because they put out these buds – which look like green spiders – that can be picked off and planted to become entirely new plants. During my school presentations, I tell the third grade science class story and make the point about using healthy forms of self-expression to deal with strong emotions. I also bring up a student from the audience and play a game that involves giving away one of the buds. I have given away over 500 plants since I started sharing this story in 2001, and I get all types of reactions. Some students e-mail me pictures of the plant months later. One girl just took the plant and said, "Where's the spider?"

The reason it is so important to express yourself in a healthy way has to do with coping skills. If you don't have healthy outlets for dealing with stress, then alcohol or other drugs can easily become your outlet. I was reminded of this during my predoctoral internship at Mount Sinai Medical Center in New York City. One of my rotations was on the Traumatic Brain Injury Unit. It was the most difficult – yet rewarding – job I have ever had. One patient who I will never forget taught me a lesson about self-expression.

E was dumped by his girlfriend one month before his high school graduation. I will call him "E" because I do not want to use his real name. He was angry and depressed. Like many high school students in that situation, he called up his friends, told them what happened, and they did the stereotypical thing – they took him out and got him drunk. E returned home around two in the morning, drunk and more emotional than before he left. Alcohol abuse intensifies emotions. If you are angry before you use, you can become really angry while intoxicated. If you are depressed before you use, you could even become suicidal once you do. I do not know if E attempted suicide that night, but I do know that he got on a motorcycle – without a helmet – and drove himself into a tree. He suffered a severe brain injury. When E awoke in the hospital, he could not move any thing on the left side of his body. He could not talk clearly and he was so confused that he kept trying to pull the tubes out of his arms. The doctors had to put restraints on him to keep him from doing so. As I watched that young man struggle through the early phases of a head injury, I learned that there are far worse things in life than death.

It took E three months to begin to walk and communicate again. I met with E every day and my job was to assess his cognitive ability and talk to him about his emotions. One day, I asked him about the night of the accident. I asked him if he wanted to hurt himself. He looked at me and said, "I don't know what happened that night, but I can tell you that there has got to be a better way to deal with getting dumped." E will probably have cognitive and physical deficits for the rest of his life, but even he understood the downside of using alcohol to cope with intense emotions.

To be good at achieving natural highs you have to be able to express yourself in a healthy way. You cannot practice emotional avoidance. The goal is to be aware of your emotions – good or bad – and to express them through healthy outlets. For me, it was sports in high school, academics, and social activism in college. Today there are about a dozen ways in which I find myself coping with stressors and emotions without turning to substances or hurting myself in other ways. Running, cooking, and listening to great music are some of my favorites today. You may choose music, acting, or hanging out with friends. No matter what you choose, it should be an activity that tends to leave you feeling better when you're done.

Exercise: Make a list of up to twenty activities that you enjoy. Pick out the items that you think would help you reduce stress and feel better following a stressful event. Next time you're stressed out look at the list and try one of the items. See if it works to help you feel better.

Book Recommendation: One of my favorite books is M. Scott Peck's *The Road Less Traveled*. Peck passed away several years ago, but he was a psychiatrist who wrote about a common problem among many of his patients – they believed that life should be easy. The problem with this thinking is life is often not easy. Peck noticed that when his patients would encounter a problem, they would rather complain about it or abuse themselves than face emotional pain. The book takes a fascinating look at the great lengths some people will go to in order to avoid emotional pain and the neuroses that develop as a result.

Brain Facts: Self-expression and Stress Management
In recent years, expressive writing has become a favorite relaxation technique for many psychologists to use with their patients. This technique has been found to have advantages over traditional treatments because it requires very little training and can be done anywhere with almost any age group.[5] A recent study of depression-vulnerable college students showed that expressive writing for 20 minutes 3 days in a row lowered symptoms of depression 6 months after the assignment.[6]

Expressive writing is believed to work by allowing the writer to express thoughts that would otherwise be suppressed. The ability to write out one's innermost thoughts and feelings can help to free the mind of those thoughts for the remainder of the day. There is a form of memory called "working memory," which temporarily stores and manipulates information – like when someone tells you a phone number. It is believed that stressful thoughts take up much of your working memory capacity, which prevents it from being used for problem solving during other daily life events. For example, if you are thinking constantly about what you are going to say to someone who really upset you, you may have higher levels of stress and less tolerance for waiting on line at the grocery store. A recent study showed that stressful thoughts and feelings are easier to deal with after a person has had a chance to free up their working memory through expressive writing.[7] So the next time you get upset, try writing about the event. Make sure you write out as many details as you feel are necessary. If it is too difficult the first time, try it again a few days later. As you go about the rest of your day or week, explore whether or not you feel any better.

Achieve Natural Highs Everyday

"I would prefer to see a Just Say No comedy [movie]. 'This summer –
Rogan and Franco are…Getting their law degrees, responsibly.'"
-Andrés du Bouchet

There are many types of proven natural highs. Running long distances releases opiates in the brain and allows runners to experience a sense of euphoria. My wife loves running – even in the dead of winter. When she goes out in the cold I tell her, "If you get lost, I'm not coming to get you." She even runs when she has a cold because she claims it makes her feel better. Personally, as an Italian-American guy living in New York City, my natural high is eating. Eating releases small amounts of the feel-good chemical dopamine into the reward center of the brain, which elevates your mood. Eating great food must release a ton of dopamine in my brain because I ate a pizza recently – at DiFara's in Brooklyn – that was so good it made me cry happy tears. There is nothing creepier than seeing a grown man eating and weeping. This book explores running and eating natural highs in more detail, but it also focuses on laughing, achieving, loving, helping others, and creating your own natural high.

Natural highs come in all shapes and sizes. Some of the best are the creative ones that few people know about. One of my favorite natural high stories occurred when I was in college. A friend of mine came in and said, "Matt, we should duct tape someone to a wall." I asked, "Where did you learn that?" He said, "Spanish TV. Telemundo." The next morning we asked a friend if she would stand on a chair in the student center and let us duct tape her to the wall. So once our friend was firmly duct taped to the wall, we pulled the chair out from underneath her and ran away. We hid around the corner and watched other students' reactions as they walked to class and saw a human being stuck to the wall. Some people freaked out, trying to poke at it and see if she was real. My favorite reaction was from students who grew up in New York City who walked by it – looked at it – and kept going. I have told that story at hundreds of schools and after I leave dozens of them have decided to duct tape the principal to the wall. In all cases, the principal was willing. One school did the duct tape activity as a fundraiser. They charged a dollar a strip and raised over $2000. I think the principal is still up there.

It is important to note that the natural highs presented in this book – if done to excess – can all be abused. For example, over one-third of children in this country suffer from obesity and the rewarding aspects of eating may play a role in that epidemic. It is also difficult for me to run in Central Park and occasionally see painfully thin women exercising. I do not know what is wrong with them, but when I see the same sickly looking person every time I am out there I suspect anorexia or exercise bulimia. I had my eyes opened to these problems by my wife – a clinical psychologist who specializes in the treatment of eating disorders. It upsets my wife so much to see a dangerously thin woman exercising that I try to lighten the mood. I just look at her and say, "Hey, at least business is good."

One key element to achieving healthy natural highs is to incorporate them into a balanced life. If any activity you enjoy interferes with your academic, social or emotional functioning then it is out of balance. It may feel amazing to fall in love and be in a new relationship, but the natural high of loving someone is not worth failing out of school for. In college, my natural high was sports. I can remember being a freshman and telling people my major was baseball. It was my honest opinion at the time, but it was naïve. If my life were just baseball in college, I would have missed out on discovering a love for science, traveling and cooking – all of which started during my undergraduate years.

Another important element to achieving healthy natural highs is avoiding internal negativity. This type of negativity can actually be a natural high blocker. I almost did it to myself on a recent three-day kayaking and camping trip to Jackson Hole, WY – a place where you can have a natural high by just opening your eyes. My friend Paul Brown –who is a real life Man versus Wild-type guy – was kayaking with me across Jackson Lake to our camp site. A few hours into our paddle trip, I start angrily swatting every fly that got near my face. I must have looked ridiculous swinging at the air while trying to keep from tipping over. It would have served me right to fall in the water because I was ruining the experience. Paul asked me what was wrong and I told him, "I hate these flies! If I stop they're going to lay eggs in my ears!" That idea came from an internet article I read about a guy who had flies lay eggs that hatched in his ear. Paul heard this and told me I needed to spend less time reading blogs and more time enjoying the real world. As I continued to whine, I realized that I was stressing myself out. Eventually I made the decision to adapt to the environment and accept the fact that in order to experience this once-in-a-lifetime natural high, I would have to accept a little discomfort. I am happy to report that I was able to calm down and enjoy one of the most memorable trips of my life. As for the flies, I eventually just let them walk all over my ears and eyeballs like everyone else does out there.

Attitude determines whether or not you will have a natural high. I remember doing a high school workshop at a conference at Glassboro College in New Jersey and one of the advisors told the group a story about sky diving. It was the perfect natural high story: 1) It involved something incredibly challenging – yet fun; 2) She took every precaution to ensure her safety, which involved hiring a highly experienced instructor; and 3) She experienced a rush of positive emotions so strong she could not wait to tell people about it as soon as it was over. Her story was uplifting until she got to the part about how when she returned home, her husband "picked and picked" at her experience, putting the whole idea down, until she did not want to talk about it anymore. Despite loving the natural high, she told us that she had never considered doing it again because of her husband's negativity.

There are so many things that can interfere with a great natural high. It can be your attitude or the attitude of the people who surround you. The one thing that is clear to me now is that you have to put in some work to achieve the natural high. It requires effort and creativity, but the payoff can change your life in a positive way. I hope after reading this book you will consider overcoming an obstacle that has prevented you from achieving a healthy natural high that you have always dreamed about.

Exercise: If you are going to duct tape someone to a wall, there are a few things to keep in mind first. 1) You cannot just take someone and stick them on a wall. You must ASK first. 2) To make this a true challenge, limit yourself to one roll of duct tape. 3) Make sure to do it on a brick or concrete wall. If you choose a wall with wallpaper, the paper will come off (not good). 4) Do not stick the person on a tree, because if you do that the person might stop breathing (definitely not good). I would recommend doing it as a competition between groups. Some schools enjoy doing it as a competition between grades. Keep in mind – it is a lot harder than you think to put someone on a wall with one roll of duct tape.

Brain Facts: Laughter versus Cocaine
In my opinion, natural highs are superior to chemical highs because they combine short term pleasure with long term benefit. In 2003, a team from Stanford University demonstrated that laughter activated the same brain regions as cocaine use.[8] Two of the areas of activation that laughter and cocaine use shared in common were the nucleus accumbens and the amygdala. These areas, together with a third area – the ventral tegmental area – make up the brain's reward system. When activated, this system is awash with dopamine. This chemical acts as a reward for the brain and plays a pivotal role in motivation to continue the behavior. Over time, drug use damages the reward center of the brain because it is being forced to release dopamine based on the dose the drug user is giving it. Natural highs use the same brain area, but the amount of dopamine released during a natural high does not damage the brain tissue. Over time the person who uses drugs will have a decreased ability to get high, while the person pursuing natural highs will not.

More Facts: Evidence for Natural Highs
The prevention literature does not use the phrase "natural highs" – rather, they prefer the terms "alternative" or "substance-free" activities. These terms are similar in that they all describe activities that are healthy and enjoyable. There have been a number of studies over the past decade suggesting that college students who hold positive attitudes towards substance-free activities and subsequently engage in them regularly tend to drink less frequently[9,10] Experimentally manipulated increases in substance-free activities – such as exercise and other creative events – leads to decreases in alcohol use.[11] In a 2006 study by Murphy, Barnett and Colby, college students

who reported drinking regularly were asked which alternatives to drinking they would consider just as enjoyable as drinking.[12] These alternatives were rated on a four point Likert scale (0 = unpleasant/ neutral to 4 = extremely pleasant), and the most highly rated responses from both genders included watching movies, playing a team sport, eating at restaurants and creative activities not otherwise specified. A significant predictor of whether or not the activity was considered "as enjoyable as drinking" was if it included two or more peers or a romantic partner.

The conclusion I've drawn from studies like these is that students who have enjoyable, affordable, and convenient alternatives to drinking may be more likely to reduce their substance use. It seems logical that students who do not use are more likely to continue that pattern if they also have activities that they rate as highly enjoyable. These statements are consistent with the conclusion of an NIAAA (National Institute of Alcohol Abuse and Alcoholism) panel that concluded colleges should offer more alcohol-free options such as coffeehouses and movies, and expanded hours for student centers and gyms.[13]

The beauty of alternative activities is that they are not exclusive to college students. High schools, middle schools and community groups can also offer similar alternatives – albeit with increased supervision. The key to creating events that will be rated as "enjoyable" is to empower young people to help create these events. The students need to take an active role in planning the events so that 1) some students take ownership over the event and show up, and 2) the activities reflect the interests of young people. For a program to succeed, it also needs to be flexible and grow with the changing interests of the students.

Don't Be Afraid to Take a Stand

"My roommate heard my idea for a drug-free group and said,
'That is social suicide.'
I just looked at him and said, 'Jason, you haven't washed
your sheets in a year – I'm not listening to you.'"
-Matt Bellace

I never thought that my high school prevention leadership training would be useful in college. Within weeks of arriving at Bucknell University, I was amazed by the intensity of the alcohol and other drug problems on campus. Bucknell was probably not much different than most colleges, but I had no other reference point. As time went on, this atmosphere made me increasingly uncomfortable. In my mind, I was faced with a choice. Either I was going to change my school and transfer, or change my school and do something about the problem. After speaking with friends and family, I decided to stay and change my school from within. That decision was the catalyst for the prevention group I founded at Bucknell in 1993 called C.A.L.V.I.N. & H.O.B.B.E.S. It stands for Creating A Lively Valuable Ingenious New Habit Of Being (at) Bucknell & Enjoying Sobriety. You probably would have guessed that though, right? The organization was based on the simple idea of having fun substance-free. We did not tell people how to live their lives. We just provided alternative late-night activities, such as bowling, bringing comedians to campus, and duct taping people to walls.

The group grew quickly and drew media attention on campus. Within a year and a half, we had over 50 regular members and events every weekend of the school year. I don't think it was so much what we did, but the fact that we enjoyed doing it together that made the difference. The defining moment for C & H came in 1994. A student was walking to class one morning and was hit and killed by a drunk driver while crossing the street on his way to class. The entire campus was devastated by the news. Students, parents and faculty were looking for answers and few were found. A few weeks later at a meeting of the Bucknell trustees (a.k.a., the guys with all the money)

I made a plea for help. I asked the trustees to consider making prevention more legitimate on campus by giving us a home. Several weeks later, I picked up the school newspaper and read the headline, "Calvin & Hobbes to Take Over Former Fraternity House."

The trustees approved a quarter of a million dollars to fix up a former fraternity house so C&H could live there. The fraternity was Sigma Phi Epsilon, which had closed due to drug and alcohol violations (shocker). I suspect the trustees wanted to send a message to other fraternity houses that they could be next. In 1996 we moved in, prompting a US News & World Report story to state, "...how times have changed."[14] The house drew national media attention and gave the group tremendous visibility on campus. Years later, Bucknell President William "Bro" Adams wrote my graduate school letter of recommendation stating, "Among (Mr. Bellace's) important contributions, none was more noticeable or consequential than the creation of the revolutionary student social and residential organization C.A.L.V.I.N. & H.O.B.B.E.S."

What do you think would happen to a co-ed substance free house on a college campus? You might suspect it would be buried in toilet paper or eggs within days, but nothing happened for some time. Then one night at around eleven o'clock, I was in my room when I heard what sounded like a large group of people. I looked outside my window and saw forty naked guys running towards the house! Yes, I counted. I thought they were going to destroy the house. What I did not know was that it was the Bucknell cross country team and their natural high was running naked on campus once a year. I ran to the front door and had an Iron Man moment where I thought, "I am going to stop them." Ok, you don't stop forty naked guys. In fact, you don't stop one naked guy. If a naked guy runs into my apartment right now, he can do whatever he wants. As I ran to the front door the first guy was running in. For some reason, I quickly got him in a head lock. The whole group stopped and the guy I was holding said, "You're holding me and I'm naked!" I did not know what to say. I should have said, "What's up, nephew?" Just then I gave the guy a hip toss and he flew backwards into his teammates behind him. I am definitely against homophobia. I think it is ignorant and wrong. But when the one naked athlete hit the other thirty nine, a moment of homophobia was realized.

I took a stand for C&H that night, but more importantly the group took a stand for natural highs on campus. We had a lot of help during the early years. The group's advisor, Bob Thomas, the coordinator of alcohol and other drug prevention at Bucknell, was a guiding force in helping us get off the ground. There were various professors and administrators that talked with me privately about their support for the group and the movement. There were also countless members of the group who sacrificed their time and energy to create a group that has lived on. Over the years it expanded its activities and even moved to a new house in the year 2000 – a house with a functional kitchen. In October 2008, C & H celebrated its 15th birthday. Today, Bucknell University is a much different place on the weekends. I suspect many students still drink and do drugs, but now there are options for those who want to be healthier. Bucknell has a late-night café, a dance club, several substance free residence halls, and many other activities every weekend paid for by the student government. I'd like to believe that C&H played a major role in influencing the decision to increase alternative activities at Bucknell.

One of the greatest accomplishments of the group has been to spread the word to other campuses. In fact, there have been at least eight colleges around the country that have since created grassroots efforts inspired by C&H, including P.E.A.N.U.T.S. at The College of New Jersey, and Thundercats at Villanova University. There could be no higher praise for me as a speaker than a student who decides to start a similar group after watching my presentation. Two recent groups – R.E.A.L. at Montclair State University and P.E.R.K.S. at William Paterson University – were both founded by students who attended T.I.G.S. and have seen me present. In fact, the president of C&H from 2007-2008 was a student named Nick Burns. He saw me speak three times as a high school student – and decided to attend Bucknell anyway.

Students often ask me how I got started in professional speaking.

It began partly as a result of C&H gaining national attention and local schools inviting me to come speak to their students. I was also very fortunate to have the support of the T.I.G.S. director who gave me the opportunity to present every year. My presentations back then were not very good, but I was always passionate about my message. In fact, it took me over a decade to find my comedic voice and to understand how to engage students.

I never knew the power of taking a stand until I applied to Ph.D. programs in clinical psychology. The competition was fierce. I interviewed at a school where there were two hundred applicants for four spots – only twenty applicants were interviewed. In the interview, the professor looked at my resume and skipped right to the paragraph about C&H. He read it and said, "Wow, this must have been hard for you!" I leaned in and said, "There were forty naked guys." We bonded over the story and I got into that school – Drexel University. What I didn't tell you was that I applied to seventeen Ph.D. programs over two years and only got into one. That was my only shot. When I got accepted, I was told by that same professor that the program needed students like me – students who were not afraid to take a stand and try something different.

Taking a stand is one of the most important elements to leading a naturally high lifestyle. It is not easy, but then again nothing worthwhile ever is easy. I hope for you that one day when you are in that moment when someone is sitting across the table and thinking, "Do we want you for this school?" or, "Do we want to give you this job?", they can say, "Yes. We want you because you were not afraid. You were not afraid to speak out against injustice. You were not afraid to stand up and be a leader. And you were not afraid to go through the good pain."

Brain Facts: Critical Periods

It is important for young people to learn how to socialize in healthy ways while they are young. If they do not, they can miss out on developing critical social skills. There is a well-known neuroscience experiment by Hubel and Wiesel that demonstrated a critical period for the development of vision. The researchers raised a monkey from birth to six months of age with one eyelid surgically shut.[15] The surgery prevented the monkey from seeing through that eye for six months. When the eye was opened it became clear to the scientists that the monkey could not see out of the eye and the blindness was irreversible. The scientists later discovered that the reason the monkey was blind was not because anything happened to the eye, but rather the area of the brain controlling vision was underdeveloped. Further studies revealed that visual deprivation in monkeys for as little as one week during the first six months of life can impair vision for life.[16] Similar rules also apply to humans.

Hubel and Weisel's work brought forth the idea of critical periods in brain development that apply to many different life functions in humans. The development of social skills, for example, also depends upon stimulation during certain developmental periods. There have been cases of infants who were abandoned in the wild, presumably raised by animals, and later returned to civilized society. They are known as feral children, and despite their ability to learn certain skills they showed permanently impaired social skills and language development.[17] One of the feral children named Wild Peter could never learn the value of money and was reported to be completely indifferent to it. This might sound like a nice attribute for a young person, but Wild Peter could never be socialized.

A more recent example involves the Harlow monkey studies of the 1960's. Two psychologists named Harry and Margaret Harlow conducted various studies in which they observed monkeys raised in isolation. They found that monkeys isolated for 6-12 months were physically healthy, but socially impaired. Their behavior often included crouching in the corner of their cages and rocking back and forth. This ritualistic behavior is similar to that which is seen in severely autistic children, and is believed to be a means for reducing anxiety. The isolated monkeys did not interact with other monkeys when given the chance. They did not fight, play, or show any sexual attraction. The authors concluded that a 6-month period of isolation during the first 18 months of life produced persistent and serious disturbances in behavior. In contrast, the isolation of an older animal for the same period of time did not have the same devastating results. Therefore, there is something vulnerable about the developing brain in that social isolation during a critical period causes irreversible changes.[18]

If we expand this thinking to adolescent social development, it might help put the concept of substance abuse prevention into a new perspective. We know that the human brain is not fully developed until age twenty-five.[19] However, my wife thinks that for men this age extends to forty-five. It is notable that the last areas of the brain to develop are those that involve complex decision making and social development. If you allow the average fifteen year old to spend weekends getting drunk or high, they may develop mechanisms that rely heavily on drugs. However, if you take the average fifteen year old and provide them with healthy ways to have fun, they are more likely to rely on those skills later on in life.

Summary
The four basic elements of leading a naturally high lifestyle include: Leaning on healthy people for support; Expressing your emotions in a healthy way; Achieving natural highs everyday; and Do not be afraid to take a stand. These four points were created partly from my experiences and partly from research on the protective factors against substance abuse. The remaining chapters of this book will describe specific natural highs, like laughing, running and eating. However, if you are considering a natural high activity that is not discussed in this book just make sure it is safe and leaves you feeling better physically and mentally then you were before you started.

CHAPTER TWO

Laughing

"YOUR BRAIN KNOWS HOW TO BALANCE A NATURAL HIGH.
YOU WILL NEVER HEAR, 'THAT MOVIE WAS SO FUNNY LAST
NIGHT, I'M HUNG OVER.'"
-MATT BELLACE

There are two forms of laughing natural highs: laughing, and making others laugh. The natural high of laughing can be such an intense experience it can make your face hurt. These are the kinds of laughs you get while watching your favorite comedian or staying up all night in middle school at a sleepover. If you have ever had this kind of natural high you know why stand-up comics refer to doing well on stage as "killing" or "destroying." Laughing can also be a subtle experience like when you see a funny cartoon that makes you smile. The Far Side cartoons always seem to do that for me, especially the one of the child entering a gifted school and pushing against a door that reads, "Pull." The other form of a laughing natural high comes from making others laugh. Comedian Jerry Seinfeld said in a 1993 interview on the Charlie Rose Show that making a large crowd of people laugh was, "The best moment I've ever felt." Making people laugh and getting paid afterwards is amazing, but you don't need to be a professional comedian to feel the high of making others laugh. If you have a good sense of humor and decent timing you can take advantage of any life situation. For example, women love jokes about their weight, and bosses are dying to know that their hair transplant looks like Vice President Joe Biden's...? Seriously, making people laugh is the best, but be careful.

One of my fondest experiences of a receiving a laughing natural high occurred while watching Bill Cosby's stand-up special "Himself" on television. I was in fourth grade and my mom rented the video for us to watch. It was the first time I saw my mother laughing so hard she cried. The crazy part was I laughed until I cried, too. Late comedian Bernie Mac reported in an interview that watching his mother cry laughing while watching Cosby made him want to become a comedian. For me, it just made me marvel that someone with nothing but a microphone could do that to people.

I was lucky enough to meet Bill Cosby in 2005. My wife purchased tickets for my birthday to see his show at the Apollo Theater in Harlem. My brother happened to be friends with Mr. Cosby's former personal assistant, so he called her and requested a post-show meet-and-greet. I went to the show with fellow comedian Joe Matarese and his father. We watched in amazement as Cosby crushed the room for two hours. Most comics can do about 30-45 minutes of strong material – two hours is like Michael Jordan level! Anyway, after the show we went up to thank him. As soon as I told him my name he said, "Take a seat over there." He finished shaking hands with everyone and then sat down with us for over half an hour – on stage – and talked about comedy. Eventually the topic of my work with students was discussed. Mr. Cosby seemed very concerned that the students at my school programs might not take me seriously because I use comedy. I assured him that I make it clear when I am making a point – mostly by dropping the mic and changing my tone of voice. The entire meeting experience was a tremendous natural high, but the funniest part was what Cosby said before we left. He told us that he was tired of today's comedians being so filthy on stage. He said, "I wish I could have a competition with these guys. They could swear and I could swear." Then he looked at us and said, "I would [expletive] destroy them!"

When it comes to laughter, I believe that it is truly better to give than to receive. Prior to becoming a comedian, I probably only made people laugh unintentionally. For example, in college I made the mistake of telling my friends that I had a fear of feminine products or "Gyno-lotro-phobia" as I called it. Of course, one of them thought it would be funny to get one of those maxi pads and stick it on my leg. In that moment of tension with everyone laughing at me, I start scraping the pad off with a paper cup and announced, "These things must really hurt when girls take them off." Looks of horror and amusement filled the faces of every female in the room. One of them said, "No, you idiot, they go on the other way!" I was like, "Yeah, I'm sure no one has ever messed that one up before."

One of my favorite things to do these days is hang out with fellow comedians and make each other laugh. Comedians spend a lot of time alone driving to gigs, but thanks to cell phones we are constantly talking to each other. We're like New York City cab drivers speaking in English. One of my favorite things to do is leave impressions on another comedian's voicemail. My only impression is Tony Soprano, but comedian Joe Matarese calls me back with Sylvester Stallone, deceased baseball announcer Harry Kallis, sports talk host Christopher "Mad Dog" Russo and many more. One of my all-time favorite messages was when I left a Tony Soprano Christmas greeting for comedian Lenny Marcus, who is Jewish. For some reason ignorant statements sound much funnier in the voice of Tony.

My wife is a great laugher, which I am very lucky for because I would hate to bomb for life. The one bit that gets her every time is when we are driving and I make up phony words to songs on the radio. Just like the voicemails, I make sure the lyrics contain a reference to something that happened recently in our lives. A song that lends itself perfectly to this is Josh Grobin's, "You Raise Me Up." It is slow, predictable and just annoying enough that she doesn't mind the interruption.

Exercise: Pick your favorite song and try to come up with words that make fun of something or someone that bothered you recently. If you hit just one or two lines well, you will get the intended effect. If you do it in front of friends and make it about them, it is even better.

Comedy = Pain + Time

*"The second time I auditioned at the Comic Strip Comedy Club
in New York City the judge came up to me afterwards and said,
'Better!' I said, 'Wow, thanks!'
She said, 'No. Last time, you were better.'"*
- Matt Bellace

In my opinion, the best laughing natural highs come from stressful situations. I think one reason humans evolved the ability to laugh was to counteract the natural lows that can happen in life sometimes. I know that many of my bits have come from my own low moments. For example, several years ago my wife went to her college reunion and returned home very upset. She said, "Matt, I don't know how to tell you this, but this weekend, I had feelings for my ex-boyfriend." I looked at her and said, "So? I had feelings for eight women today. Two were on T.V., one was in an e-mail."

That joke is one of my favorites because it is so honest. It was actually a very painful experience to have her come home from a weekend away and share those feelings. It was not instant comedy, but once a few months had passed – and our relationship survived – it became fodder. Time has a way of giving you a perspective on life. More importantly, if you are going to go through all that it takes to be a stand-up comedian, you had better believe in what you are saying. Talk about something that matters to you and something that moved you.

Laughter is also a great coping mechanism for dealing with life's little irritations. I was on a flight to San Francisco and was happy about getting the aisle seat. "It's quicker to the bathroom and easier to stick my legs out," I thought. What I didn't realize is that the aisle seat is a 5-hour butt and genital parade on my shoulder. The whole flight I heard, "Oh, I'm so sorry," while feeling strangers rub themselves on me like a bear marking a tree in the woods. At one point, I felt anatomy on my face. I don't know what part it was, but it was disturbing. Just once I wish the airlines could produce an honest safety video saying, "We are sorry, but if you're sitting in an aisle seat you may need a tissue."

Exercise: Write down a painful or embarrassing life event that you are comfortable sharing with others. Do not write down every detail, just the most powerful elements. After a revealing statement consider adding a punch line. For example, "Getting dumped was the most painful moment of my life, almost as bad as watching the movie Norbit." Once you've got a solid story with a couple of punch lines, read it to a friend or post it online and see what other people think.

Brain Facts: Laughter

A recent study showed that laughing activates the same brain areas as using cocaine. The study was performed by Mobbs and colleagues (2003) and it presented 42 "funny" and 42 "unfunny" cartoons drawn by Bizarro cartoonist Dan Piraro.[1] One funny cartoon showed a man sitting on a deserted island looking malnourished and dirty with a bizarre looking creature sitting next to him. The caption – from the creature – read, "If I have to spend one more day on this island, I am going to start hallucinating." Of course, you would expect the man to be hallucinating about the creature not the other way around, which makes the cartoon amusing. It is not exactly laugh out loud funny, but it generated a smile from me the first time I saw it. The unfunny cartoon is the same man, except there is no creature and now the caption is coming from the man. There is really nothing remotely funny about the second one – it is simply a realistic thought. These cartoons were shown to healthy volunteers while their brains were scanned in a functional MRI (fMRI) machine that measures changes in blood flow across brain tissue. Participants were asked to press a button to indicate something as either as "funny" or "unfunny." Comparing each person's "funny" brain scan to their "unfunny" brain scan, scientists were able to show that when something is perceived as funny the reward center of the brain is activated. As its name implies, the reward center of the brain plays an important role in the processing of rewarding events. Previous studies have also shown that the reward center is activated during cocaine induced highs.[2]

The knowledge about the reward center of the human brain comes mostly from research on the rat brain. The chemistry of the human brain and the rat brain are similar and it is believed that the process of drug addiction may be the same for both. The cocaine and amphetamine reward system includes neurons that use dopamine. They are found in a part of the brain called the ventral tegmental area (VTA) in the brain stem, which are connected to the nucleus accumbens and other areas such as the prefrontal cortex. The VTA and the nucleus accumbens are two structures involved in the reward system for all drugs, including alcohol and tobacco, although additional mechanisms might be involved for specific drugs.

I am not going to argue that laughing is a more intense high than cocaine, but the brain knows how to balance a natural high. You will never hear, "That movie was so funny last night, I'm hung over." Laughter is a superior high on many levels. The health benefits from laughter include improved immune functioning, stress relief, increased pain tolerance, and improved cardiovascular health.[3,4] Personally I have gained psychological benefits from laughter, including reducing anxiety, bonding with other people in a shared experience, and improved mood.

Getting the Joke

"I'm a truffle away from being Will from Will and Grace"
- Matt Bellace

The toughest part of receiving laughter as a natural high is that you have to get the joke. The understanding of comedy has a mysterious quality to it because it is one part intelligence, one part social awareness and at least a little sense of humor. I knew I had what it took from an early age because my second grade teacher, Mrs. Marks, told my mother, "Matthew is the only student who gets all of my jokes." I was probably just an awful kiss up from an early age, but at least I knew when to laugh.

You may not realize it, but there are unspoken social rules about laughter. I love Joe Pesci's famous scene in the movie *Goodfellas*. A recent search on YouTube.com titles this scene "Funny Guy." It takes place in a night club and all these mobsters are sitting around laughing out loud at Pesci's character, who is telling a funny story. Ray Liotta's character – in a very complimentary way – calls him a "funny guy." Pesci's mood quickly gets dark and he becomes belligerent towards Liotta's character. He repeatedly asks him in angrier and angrier tones, "You think I'm funny? What makes me so funny?" The tension builds to the verge of violence until Pesci's character and the entire table erupts into laughter. The scene is so memorable partly because it violates our perception of what is supposed to happen when people are laughing. Laughter is believed to have evolved as a way to let the others in the group know that everything is safe. The *Goodfellas* scene does not turn violent. However, the mere suggestion of violence during a humorous moment is so unusual – yet fitting for anti-social criminals – that it instantly became part of American pop culture history.

In elementary school, it did not require much to get a good laugh going. Of course, no one can blame a kid for being so giddy when any given school day might involve using the gym class parachute. I recently watched kindergarten kids stand in a circle, grab the end of the parachute and shake like bobble head dolls. There is no drug ever made that could match the feeling of the gym class parachute. I used to love it when they would let a kid run underneath. Someone would scream, "Doesn't Timmy have anxiety problems?" That's when you knew it was getting good.

In middle school, all I needed for a great laugh were my friends and a sleepover. Take some pizza add a little sleep deprivation and somehow you would unlock the comedian in all of us. Suddenly, around 3 AM the kid who threw his farts like Spiderman looked like a comic genius. The more tired we got, the funnier everything seemed. It was almost like our brains hit a point where they could relax and then would start making all crazy-funny associations. It is those random associations that lend themselves so well to laughter.

Of course, getting the joke requires that the associations are funny to others, which means you need to share a common language. For example, after a show one day a student came up to me and said,

"You look like that actor Eric McCormack." I had no idea who that was, so it did not seem funny to me. As soon as I got home, I Googled him and found out that he played Will in the sitcom Will and Grace. So now the truffle joke – listed at the top of this section – is actually part of my act. Of course, the only people who laugh are those familiar with the show. In a decade it will probably be as funny to young people as an Alex P. Keaton reference is to them today.

Exercise: Plan an old school sleep over with friends. If you think you're too old for it then try a road trip, an outdoor adventure weekend, or a vacation house. It doesn't matter what you do, just make sure it involves hanging out late at night with good friends and see if you can have a laughing natural high.

Interview with Comedians: Getting the Joke
In preparing this chapter, I interviewed a few of New York City's finest working stand-up comedians about their first experiences watching stand-up comedy. All of them reported that it took place while they were young and it obviously had a profound effect on their choice of profession. The comedians I spoke to were: Ted Alexandro who has appeared on The Late Show with David Letterman, Conan O'Brien and Comedy Central Presents; Dave Siegel who has appeared on Comedy Central's Laugh Riots; Moody McCarthy who has appeared on Last Comic Standing and Jimmy Kimmel Live; and Joe Matarese who has appeared on The Late Show with David Letterman and Comedy Central Presents.

Ted Alexandro
"As a kid, I listened to all of my parents' comedy albums. It was such an intimate experience because there was no image to watch – just sound to engage my entire imagination. It was so appealing to me – not just the laughter, but the pauses. Here was this person who was speaking to a room full of people, commanding their attention to the point where they would listen intently even when he wasn't being funny. The comic that stands out the most early on was Steve Martin, but in high school it was Eddie Murphy."

Dave Siegel

"I grew up in Woodmere, New York on Long Island. In the summer, my parents would take me to the Westbury Music Fair. I remember watching Rodney Dangerfield and Jackie Mason perform. I'm sure most of their jokes went over my head, but I remember seeing a bit about baseball players adjusting their crotch at home plate. As a huge baseball fan I completely related to it and laughed hysterically. It was so good that as soon as I got home I had to immediately start telling my friends the joke."

Moody McCarthy

"It was while watching Richard Pryor tapes and seeing the guy totally in command of a large group of people. I was twelve years old – didn't get all of the jokes – but had fun watching my brothers in awe of him. It was completely intimidating to watch Pryor. I never thought, 'I could do that.'"

Joe Matarese

"I guess like a lot of comics my age, it was listening to Steve Martin. I grew up in Cherry Hill, New Jersey and was about eleven or twelve when I would get together with a neighbor and listen to albums in the basement. Listening to stand-up comedians also became a way for me to connect with my father. Listening to albums together would help me feel closer to him – I still do it today, but now it's with clips on YouTube."

Making Others Laugh

> *"The Four Levels of Comedy:*
> *Make your friends laugh, make strangers laugh, get paid to*
> *make strangers laugh, and make people talk like you*
> *because it's so much fun."*
> *-Jerry Seinfeld*

Do you think you're funny? Do you believe you could get up and make a room full of people laugh? The philosophy of the Manhattan

Comedy School in New York City is that anyone can learn stand-up comedy and perform a five-minute set. I agree. Andy Engle, its founder, runs the school out of Comix Comedy Club and takes students from their first joke to a performance at a comedy club. Comedy classes are truly the first rung on the entertainment ladder, but I know from experience that they can be a lot of fun.

One benefit of taking a comedy class is social support. The environment of comedy classes tends to be very supportive, which is what you will need to combat the full on self-esteem assault known as stand-up comedy. One of the most supportive experiences I ever had in my life occurred as a result of taking a stand-up comedy class at Camden Community College in Blackwood, NJ. The final exam was a performance at a hole-in-the-wall "comedy club" called Bonkers Comedy Café. I'm not kidding about the hole-in-the-wall part, because behind the stage was a four foot hole in the wall that led to a huge room below that was under construction. If you leaned against the curtain the wrong way, you could fall 30 feet down on to rubble.

The favorite memory of the whole night was the intro music that our "teacher" (who was not remotely funny) played before each act. It was Eddie Money's cheesy 1980's song, "I Think I'm love." Do yourself a favor and either download a 30-second free clip of this miserable song or check out the song during the ending credits of the Kevin James movie Paul Blart Mall Cop. Imagine eight comedians – introduced one after the other – and then start and stop the song mid-lyric. He never even bothered to restart the song, so you would just hear, "Give it up for your next up comedian Vince Valentine, '.....I think I'm in love, and my life's....'" and then Vince would begin his set.

My classmates and I were all so nervous about performing for the first time that none of us even acknowledged the hole, the rubble below, or the lame music. Our anxiety was understandable since we were performing in front of our friends and family. I know veteran comics who still get nervous performing in front of their loved ones. However, the experience bonded us because there was this sense that we were all in it together. In many ways, that is why I love being a stand-up comic in New York City. There is an unspoken bond that we are all in this together. It may sound silly, but the perception of that kind of support has freed me to try jokes I would never try without it.

It has been over seven years since the class, but I still keep in touch with two of my fellow classmates. One of them is Caroline Murphy, a mother of three who took the class to try something new. To be honest, when I first met her she was overweight and looked fairly depressed. She was so nervous the first time she stood up to perform in class it made me uncomfortable. But over the eight week course, Caroline underwent a transformation. There was something about the support of strangers and the high of getting laughs that seemed to motivate her. By the night of the performance, she had lost weight, was more confident and when she got on stage, she blew us away! Not only was she funny, but inspirational as well.

Several years later, Caroline wrote to me and told me about her battle with a brain tumor. She was recovering and wanted to return to stand-up to try to recapture some of those great feelings. I was so honored that she had taken the time to get in touch with me and share her story. The truth is we only knew each other for a couple of months, but the bond had remained. In her mind, I was a positive and supportive influence at a crucial time in her life. We all need those people we can turn to for unconditional support, but it feels even better to be one of those people who can provide the unconditional support.

Exercise: If you really want to be a comedian I would recommend taking a stand-up comedy workshop or improvisation class near you. If you live close to New York City and you choose stand-up, I recommend Andy Engel's Manhattan Comedy School (www. manhattancomedyschool.com). If you live near Philadelphia, I recommend the Philadelphia Comedy Academy (www. philadelphiacomedyacademy.com), and if you live in between I recommend the Stress Factory Comedy Class (www.stressfactory.com) in New Brunswick, New Jersey. Classes tend to be a commitment of several weeks and two or three hundred dollars, but it will definitely expand your horizons, improve your speaking skills and give you a safe environment in which to perform. During the class, you can also really compare the natural high of giving laughter and receiving laughter. You may even meet some friends in the process.

Interview with Comedians: Giving the Laugh
When I asked other comedians about their first time telling jokes – not surprisingly – many were hooked from the very beginning. In fact, some involved re-telling jokes from legendary comedians' acts. I have a theory that imitation is the only way to start developing your own style in comedy. It sounds like a contradiction, but when you are trying to do something so completely unique that no one around you can do it, you have got to start somewhere. I doubt there was a high school shortstop playing baseball in New Jersey – or in any state – in the early 90's who did not try and imitate "The Wizard of Oz" Ozzie Smith.

Ted Alexandro
"There was this girl Karen in fourth grade that I would trade Steve Martin lines with every day. I guess her parents let her listen to their albums, too. I was always in search of that person who really knew the lines. You didn't want some guy making a half-assed attempt at the jokes. It felt so good when you could just go back and forth and get the feel of what it is was like to tell the joke."

Dave Siegel
"I never really wanted to do anything else. My first show was at the Comic Strip in New York City. It didn't go well, but my next one was at Gotham. It went really well and I was hooked."

Moody McCarthy
"Before I performed for the first time, I wrote jokes on my own for over a year. I didn't tell anyone. The first time I performed I went to a local open mic with two of my friends and it went well. It was like Fools Gold, though, because most comics bomb the first time out.

Getting a laugh is the best feeling. Even after all these years, I love the feeling of telling a new joke and getting a positive reaction."

Joe Matarese

"In the beginning you don't realize that you're not good. The first laughs you get feel amazing! It is addicting like a drug. I felt euphoric and for the first time in my life I thought, 'I could be good at this.'"

For the Love of the Game

*"When I started doing stand-up I remember
rushing home from work, skipping dinner and getting dressed
all so I could perform at an open mic.
My wife yelled at me, 'Why are you doing this to yourself?'
I just looked at her and said, 'You're right. I should quit psychology.'"*
- Matt Bellace

The hardest part of traveling the country and making others laugh is the uncertainty of the career. No one can tell you how long it will take to become a comedian – if it ever happens. Once you are a comedian, no one can tell you how long it will be before you get on television – if you get on at all. I consider myself extremely fortunate. My career has been described as a "hybrid" career where I get to tell jokes, but also get to motivate students in the process. It also happens to be a lot more stable than performing every night at the Ha Ha Hole. Do not get me wrong – the clubs are where comedians are born and they are great fun. However, they are a difficult place to work at long-term, while still maintaining your physical and mental health.

One of the keys to living naturally high in your life – no matter what your career – is having a passion for what you do. It is a lot more difficult to get into trouble when you are focused on working hard and accomplishing things. The great thing about comedy is there is a never ending amount of work to be done. Your act is never "finished" – there are always more jokes to be written, more exploration to be done. As I look back at my very early days of trying to make people laugh, I realize that my work was beginning long before I ever stepped on stage.

One problem I had to overcome before I could do comedy was convincing others that what I was saying was meant to be funny – not mean. The first thing I had to realize was that my facial expressions were always the same when telling a joke. That is fine if you are Steven Wright or Norm MacDonald, but I was not. My straight faced delivery would leave some people looking at me and thinking, "Wow, what a jerk!" Fortunately, a friend of mine clued me into this – of course, I felt horrible because I was just trying to be funny. So, as I learned more about the finer points of comedy, I began making my punch lines more obvious with a slight change in my tone of voice or an exaggerated facial expression. Things improved very quickly. It was a turning point for me because you always have to "sell" the joke, which means you have to subtly indicate that you are kidding.

I also learned not to rely on jokes that attack people, especially those with physical or mental problems. When I was five years old, our house painter called asking for my parents. I picked up and asked this nice – albeit large – man, "Why are you so fat?" He was so nice about it, too. He never got upset. If I was him, I probably would have responded, "Because five year olds are so delicious." Honestly, I was probably just mimicking the negative things I heard about fat people from my father. Recently, my dad was standing outside of Cold Stone Creamery, staring in and watching people eat their ice cream. He looks back at me and says, "Look at those people eat all that fat! Isn't that something?" I was like, "Yeah, dad, it's called happiness."

By seventh grade, I still hadn't learned my lesson. I got caught in history class drawing a funny cartoon mocking a classmate – CJ DeYoung. Do you know him? CJ would always hit on girls in our class. By mid-year, he must have asked out half the girls in our grade and it wasn't because he was so good at it. The cartoon happened to be pretty funny, but the problem was that our history teacher happened to be CJ's mother. I can still remember the feeling I got as she swiped the cartoon out of my hand. To her credit, she remained fairly calm, but I felt like I had just kidnapped her child.

I had no one to blame. It was my fault and I was being mean. It was a lesson that I still remember to this day – there are actually rules in comedy.

For those who love comedy so much they wish to pursue it as a career, there are many paths the career can take. This chapter focused heavily on stand-up, but there is also comedic acting like in sketch comedy or improvisation. Many comedians go on to become writers for television talk shows and sitcoms. For those lucky enough to make it as performers on television, the sky is the limit. Comedy has launched the careers of so many television and movie stars over the years, including Jerry Seinfeld, Eddie Murphy, Jim Carey, Kevin James, and Chris Rock.

I love the art of stand-up comedy more now than ever. I appreciate and support comedians who do it well. In recent years, colleges, high schools and community groups have asked me to do comedy shows in the evenings. For example, the Municipal Alliance of Morris County hosted me for a day of speaking programs followed by an evening "natural high comedy event." That type of synergy is a true carry-over of my message beyond the school day. The event was great because there was funding to bring out a few of my fellow comedian friends to perform with me. The only difference between a typical comedy show in a club and one of these "natural high" events, is that the comedians are a bit cleaner and do not glamorize alcohol or other drug abuse to get laughs.

Natural High Event Idea: If you are a highly motivated social activist-type like me, you might consider putting on a natural high comedy night in your area. It could be a show for students, adults, or both, but they are great fun. You can hold it in a local comedy club and let them run it, or you can find the comedians yourself. This may sound difficult, but thanks to the internet comedians can be viewed and booked online. Just make sure you pick comedians that are comfortable doing cleaner material.

Summary

Laughter is the purest form of a natural high. People of all ages can benefit from the physical and psychological effects of laughter. Laughing releases the neurotransmitter called dopamine in the reward center of the brain and gives a sense of euphoria. If you love the natural high of laughter, you may wish to pursue it as a career in stand-up or comedic acting. To make it in this career, you will need a passion for the art of comedy and a strong work ethic. There are many sacrifices to making it as career comedian, but is giving up a 9-5 job really a sacrifice?

CHAPTER THREE

Running

"YOU HAVE TO STAY IN SHAPE. MY GRANDMOTHER...STARTED WALKING FIVE MILES A DAY WHEN SHE TURNED 60. SHE'S 97 TODAY AND WE DON'T KNOW WHERE SHE IS."
-ELLEN DEGENERIS

In eighth grade I used to wake up at 6 AM and run three miles before school. It was self-inflicted torture – like making your own bed at a hotel. Any dedicated runner would probably call my routine a day off, but I was in training to be the greatest middle school athlete the world had ever seen. Unfortunately, there was no award for a young athlete with shockingly large eyebrows or I would have won hands down. My morning runs were a natural high. I can still remember how great it felt to sit in class on the mornings I ran. My mood was more positive and my energy level was through the roof. I actually had a better attitude about doing school work. Typically, I had the "I don't need math, I'll use a calculator" mindset. But something about having more energy in class makes you feel like you can do anything.

As an athlete in high school, however, running was served up as punishment for a bad performance. We only ran when we were forced to run so I avoided it. In graduate school, I rediscovered running for pleasure because I was too poor to join a gym and in need of a healthy coping mechanism to deal with stress. I met my soon-to-be wife in graduate school and she is a real runner. She was on the cross country and track teams at Colgate University (Hamilton,

NY) and even today can run for like ten miles at mid-six minute pace per mile. She runs almost every day during all seasons. She has a saying, "There is no such thing as bad weather, just bad clothing." My saying to her in the dead of winter is, "If you freeze or get lost out there, I'm not coming to get you."

I used to think my wife was crazy for running in the winter. I had a dozen reasons why I would never do it. I used to think it was bad to run in the cold until I read that humans can tolerate running in freezing cold much better than they can in sizzling hot conditions. I used to think that running while sick was ridiculous until I read that as long as you do not have a respiratory infection or the flu, running actually makes you feel better even if it does not improve the condition. Thanks to my wife's encouragement, I now try to run at least twice a week and in almost any weather. My knee surgery has slowed me down a bit, but my favorite is running during the winter in Central Park. I love how the sky turns into an unbelievable turquoise color and the air is so crisp and clean it's like you're almost not in New York City. To think that for so many years I prevented myself from achieving such a great natural high because of my own negativity and ignorance.

One of the most important elements to achieving natural highs is to keep an open mind. Ultimately, enjoying life is about positive risk taking. Aleta Meyer, a prevention expert from the National Institute on Drug Abuse, stresses the importance of positive risk taking for healthy development. She feels that without constructive challenges, young people will fulfill their risk taking needs by turning to substance abuse or unhealthy natural highs like speeding in a car or high risk sexual activity. Encouraging people to take on positive risks through activities like running or trying out for sports teams pushes personal limits and can help fill emotional needs.

Natural High Event: New Year's Eve Midnight Run
One of the healthier ways to ring in the New Year is to attend the New Year's Eve Midnight Run through Central Park in New York City. New Year's Eve has become synonymous with getting chemically high, so what better way to be a non-conformist than to

go for a run? The race kicks off with fireworks as the ball drops and the atmosphere is more of a party than a race. There are costumes, dancing and lots of noise makers during this fun-filled four-mile run. For more information, check out www.nyrr.org.

The Running Cure

"A run on a crisp 20 degree day in Central Park
is my natural high. I don't need a beer."
- Dara Bellace, PhD

By far, one of the greatest things about running in Central Park is the opportunity to see so many different people. Achilles, a worldwide organization that enables people with all types of disabilities to participate in athletics, is one of the most prominent groups in the park. If you arrive at the right time on a Saturday or Sunday morning at the 90th and Fifth Ave entrance to Central Park, you will see Achilles members preparing their wheelchairs for exercise. The chairs are not the typical wheel chairs. They are the Orange County Choppers of wheel chairs. They have chairs you can peddle with your hands, chairs with chrome wheels and even chairs that allow you to lie completely flat. My favorite is this one guy who goes out in a basic old wheel chair. He does not look impressive until he starts up a big hill. I have seen this guy at least a dozen times pushing himself – in reverse – up hills! I don't care how lazy or down I am feeling that day, seeing him motivates me to keep going.

The other running group in Central Park that always fascinates me is a group from Odyssey House. These are individuals in recovery from substance abuse who are taking part in an innovative treatment community. Odyssey House uses running to encourage former heroin, cocaine, and crack addicts to stay clean. The whole thing sounded like a bit from my stand-up act when I first read about it.[1] However, the first time I watched an Odyssey House guy run by me I didn't think it was a joke anymore. I shouldn't have assumed that my clean liver would give me breakaway speed. Odyssey House has produced some serious runners. In fact, they routinely enter around fifteen people into the New York City Marathon each fall.

The use of running to treat addiction has received increasing amounts of attention from researchers. A study conducted at Butler Hospital in Rhode Island found that outpatient treatment for alcoholism that included 12 weeks of aerobic conditioning increased the likelihood of remaining sober.[2] This makes sense given that endurance training has been shown to have a variety of positive psychological effects, including stress reduction, improved mood, and reduced pain perception. In a sense, the runners' high can replace chemical highs while acting as a healthier coping mechanism for stress.

Exercise: Take some time to read about the history and innovative treatment going on at Odyssey House. It all began in 1966 as a pilot research program at Metropolitan Hospital in New York City. They started out treating heroin abusers and quickly grew into one of the country's first drug-free therapeutic communities. For more information, go to www.odysseyhouseinc.org.

Brain Facts: The Runners' High

"I've definitely had the runners' high. It's that feeling you get after a few miles when you actually feel better. It is counter intuitive to feel better. As a comedian, I would say comedy is a better high though – probably because I can't make a living as a runner."
- Moody McCarthy

The concept of the runners' high sounds like an oxymoron. How can you get a high from doing something that causes you physical stress? Runners who have experienced the high describe feelings of euphoria and reduced pain sensation. You may have even heard that the runners' high is caused by endorphins. Well, the creepy voice in your head is right. In the 1980's, a study showed that vigorous physical activity causes a release of endorphins from the brain into the bloodstream. For years, scientists just assumed that somehow those endorphins – which come from the brain's pituitary gland – made their way back to the brain and created a sensation of euphoria. It turns out that this assumption was not correct.

In a recent study, neuroscientists were able to demonstrate that the endorphins released by the pituitary gland do not return to the brain once they have been released into the body.[3] The reason they do not make it back is because of the blood-brain-barrier, which acts like a screen to prevent large molecules from passing from the blood supply in the body to the blood supply of the brain. So if the pituitary endorphins are not able to make it back to the brain, then what was causing the high?

Well, the study showed that endorphins were being released locally (i.e., from the cortex of the brain) and were binding to opioid receptors in the frontal lobe and limbic system of the brain. That meant that the brain was releasing neurotransmitters for the primary reason of creating the sensation of euphoria. The prior studies did not have the technology to examine the active brain of a runner – they simply were using blood tests. The positron emission tomography (PET) scanner made it possible to measure opiate receptors in the brain with a scan.

Interviews with Runners: The Runners' High
To learn more about the natural high of running, I interviewed runners with a variety of experience. It may surprise you to learn that all of them reported achieving the runners' high, but what it takes them to get it varied. Dara Bellace is my wife and a former Division I cross country runner with over twenty years of running experience. Katie Heineken is a marathon runner with five marathons under her belt (and the ironic name in a book like this).

Dara Bellace
"Running allows me to feel free and strong. It is very empowering to just get away from it all and get outside for a run. After a long run, I feel accomplished, drained, and enjoy a good kind of soreness. I also feel more productive when I return to work. Even if I can run for twenty five minutes, I feel more energized and clear headed. Also,

the high I get from running has only gotten better for me as time goes by and my life has gotten busier."

Katie Heineken

"I have had natural highs from running, but it is not the same since I started running marathons. In the New York City Marathon, I got one while crossing the Queensboro Bridge, entering Manhattan and hearing everyone cheering. In general, running helps me focus more at work, gives me a sense of accomplishment, and a great appetite. I also love how it feels to take a shower after a run. I feel cleaner for some reason."

Are We Even Meant to Run?

In a chapter on how the brain gets high on running, we need to ask – are we even meant to run? Harvard Anthropologist Daniel Lieberman thinks the answer is yes. He presented his theories in the 2007 Harvard Museum of Natural History's spring lecture series titled, "Evolution Matters." Hopefully you live in a town in America where evolution still matters. I've visited some towns that evolution skipped over.

Dr. Lieberman's talk focused on the fact that even though more than one million humans run marathons worldwide each year, we are not animals typically associated with being good runners. Antelopes and cheetahs are built for speed and they've got humans beat, but horses and dogs are built more for distance and are not as good as humans. Although the equines and canines will run marathon-type distances if forced to do it, neither one does it as efficiently as humans. According to Dr. Lieberman, "Humans are terrible athletes in terms of power and speed, but we're phenomenal at slow and steady. We're the tortoises of the animal kingdom."

Dr. Lieberman believes that the appearance about two million years ago of physical adaptations that make humans better runners coincided with them eating meat. That is right, long before vegans ever existed humans were meat-seeking scavengers. It is believed that eating meat – among other things – helped us to develop tendons in our legs and feet that act like large elastic bands, storing energy and releasing it with each running stride. Our bodies also developed the ability to remain stable while running, aided by our big butt muscles and an elastic ligament in our neck to keep our head stable. Dr. Lieberman also believes that our ability to lose large amounts of heat generated while running is due to our hairlessness, our ability to sweat, and the fact that we breathe when we run. He stated, "We can run in conditions that no other animal can run in. Most animals would develop hyperthermia – heat stroke in humans – after about 10 to 15 kilometers." Dr. Lieberman envisions an evolutionary scenario where humans began eating meat as scavengers, which allowed them to run faster to the site of a fresh kill. Evolution likely favored better runners until weapons made running less important.

If the evolution lesson above does not convince you that humans were meant to run, then go watch an episode of The Biggest Loser. The contestants on the show are essentially training to be endurance athletes. The fact that they start out as the complete opposite of that only makes the show more compelling. Honestly, the show overdoes it by promoting an unhealthy level of overexercise and some horrific body shots, but the point is still made. If morbidly obese people can train themselves to run, then so can you.

Interview with Runners: Born to Run?
I asked our runners about their early experiences with running and what it was like for them to pick up the sport. It was amazing for me to learn how difficult it was for them the first time they ran.

Dara Bellace
"The first time I ran was with my dad. I was thirteen years old. I ran one mile and was totally out of breath. He wanted to talk to me during the run, but as I gasped for air I tried to tell him, 'I can't run and talk at the same time!' I must have looked ridiculous because I was running in a big winter jacket. When I finished I vowed never to run again."

Katie Heineken

"I grew up in Connecticut and started running my junior year in high school to get in better shape. I would walk / run with my dad and could only run in short bursts. I never would have started if it wasn't for my dad because I was struggling and had difficulty breathing. When I moved to New York City, I wanted a sense of community so I joined the Harriers [a running club]. I ran a half marathon and then my first marathon soon after that."

Getting Started

Bob Glover, director of the New York Road Runners Club Running Classes, has been using the following program since 1978 to train beginner runners. Before you start, make sure you see your doctor for a physical examination, have a quality pair of running shoes, and set aside a regularly scheduled time to run. If you can walk briskly for 20 minutes without stopping to rest or becoming excessively fatigued, you are ready to go. If you can't, work up to that level, taking as much time as you need.

Week	Workout (in minutes)	Total Run Time (in minutes)
1	Run 1, Walk 2 (repeat 7 times)	7
2	Run 2, Walk 2 (repeat 5 times)	10
3	Run 3, Walk 2 (repeat 4 times)	12
4	Run 5, Walk 2 (repeat 3 times)	15
5	Run 6, Walk 1 ½ (repeat 3 times)	18
6	Run 8, Walk 1 ½ (repeat 2 times)	16
7	Run 10, Walk 1 ½ (repeat 2 times)	20
8	Run 12, Walk 1, Run 8	20
9	Run 15, Walk 1, Run 5	20
10	Run 20 Nonstop	20

Interview with Runners: Advice on Running

Dara Bellace

"Running is hard on the body. It feels awkward at first, especially if you do not know how to run. I would suggest you slowly increase your mileage. Never increase your mileage by more than ten percent each week. Anyone can build up to running longer distances, but it definitely helps to run with other people or prepare for a race that has some meaning. One of my favorites was running in the 2000 Philadelphia Half Marathon with Team In Training, an organization that helps to raise money for the Leukemia and Lymphoma Society."

Katie Heineken

"I would say pace yourself – slow and steady. Do one mile, then walk before trying to run more. Don't mentally and physically defeat yourself by trying to do too much. Give yourself a reward each time you run, like having some extra ice cream that day or something. Also, it is great if you can socialize while running. I look forward to running more when I know I'm going out to run with a friend."

Exercise: If you would like more tips on the how to get into the sport of running, check out The Running Company's website, www.therunningcompany.net. If you live near a major city on the East Coast you can visit on of their many stores in person and get info on the right clothes, shoes, and routes for your running needs. Another website that is pretty cool is www.mapmyrun.com. You can map a run anywhere and figure out how far it is before you go out. If you're ready for a road race, then check out the Susan G. Komen for the Cure runs at www.komen.org.

Cleveland Surfers

This chapter could have been called a lot of things. It could have been called kayaking, hiking, skate boarding, biking, or just about anything that elevates the heart rate for more than twenty minutes. It just so happens that the natural high of running is well-researched, inexpensive, and popular, which makes it perfect for this chapter. However, one of my favorite New York Times stories in 2006 was about surfers on Lake Erie in Cleveland. That's right, Ohio. There is a small group of dedicated individuals who surf Lake Erie when the surfing is good, which happens to only be in the winter. This practice is not as unusual as you might think. I read a similar story in the Wall Street Journal in 2001 about a group of winter surfers in Cape Cod, and another recently in Minnesota who surf Lake Superior. In both cases, these individuals use special wet suits made for extreme cold water. They also surf together to watch each other for signs of hypothermia. The benefit of surfing in the winter is all about wind, which can create waves on Lake Erie that get up to 10 feet high! The waves are not the cool California ones that break slowly in long tubes. Instead the waves on Lake Erie look more like haystacks that crash quickly into icy water. This sport has some danger associated with it, but by all accounts is pretty safe with the right clothing and precautions. You may be asking yourself, "Why would people ever do this?" Well, my favorite quote was from Cleveland surfer Bill Weeber, who said, "Surfing Lake Erie is basically disgusting. But then I catch that wave and I forget about it, and I feel high all day."

I will admit that until I read the article about the Cleveland surfers, I never really attempted to surf – in cold or warm water. But the image of people with icicles hanging out of their noses paddling out in survival suits motivated me. It didn't motivate me to fly to Cleveland – I don't know how much money that would take – it motivated me to take surfing lessons during a speaking trip to San Diego.

For less than $100, I had a private lesson with a former pro surfer at the Pacific Beach Surf School (www. pacificbeachsurfschool. com). The lesson included a surf board and the tightest wetsuit ever invented. Seriously, it sucked in my gut so much I looked like a ten year old. My instructor was Ali, a four-foot-ten-inch South American former Billabong-sponsored surfer. She had given up the pro surfing gig to make some real money teaching pale guys from New York City how to fall gracefully off a surf board. If you are considering surfing, I cannot tell you how invaluable it was to spend the hour out in the water with Ali. She showed me tips and surfed along side of me to make sure I got up. Falling did make up ninety percent of my lesson, but eventually I was able to catch a wave right and stand up! Words cannot describe the surge of adrenaline that I felt that day. It was amazing and I cannot wait to do it again.

Exercise: What is your "running" type natural high? Do you snow board, surf, skate board, play tennis, basketball or something else? If you have an exercise natural high that you enjoy, do you do it as much as you would like to? If not, consider adding something else to your repertoire. Perhaps reconsider a physical activity that you had previously dismissed as "not for you." Make a list of the positive and negative things about the activity. Then ask yourself if the reasons for not trying it could be overcome, either by wearing better clothing or just developing a different perspective – like I did by starting to run in the cold weather.

Summary
The runners' high is much more than just the release of opiates from one part of the brain to the other. The experience of a natural high during a run seems to vary from feelings of everyday accomplishment, stress relief, to the exhilaration of completing a marathon. The runners' high also comes from much more than just running since there are dozens of activities that can challenge your body and your mind in the outdoors. The key is trying out many different activities that involve exercise in order to see which one is best suited for you. If there is one thing to learn from runners is that with time and effort you will get stronger and more confident. If your natural high activity does not bring you a high the first time, try, try again.

CHAPTER FOUR

Eating

"THE PIG IS AN AMAZING ANIMAL. YOU FEED A PIG AN APPLE
AND IT MAKES BACON. LET'S SEE MICHAEL PHELPS DO THAT.
PIGS ARE THE GREATEST RECYCLING MACHINES EVER."
- JIM GAFFIGAN

Growing up as an Italian American in New Jersey, I had many
opportunities to enjoy great food. Whether it was eating a slice of
Papa Tony's pizza in Cedar Grove, a Jersey Mike's Italian sub in Point
Pleasant or my grandma's rigatoni with meatballs in Collingswood,
I ate well. The only problem is that I didn't appreciate how great I
had it until it was gone. My parents would probably describe me
an incredibly picky eater who insisted on eating the same things
over and over again. In middle school, I ate Peanut Butter and Jelly
everyday for lunch. I call it PB&J OCD. It wasn't until I went to
college in Pennsylvania that I realized the rest of the world does not
eat like my family. I was truly miserable. It was the Dark Ages of
food for me.

Eating raises blood sugar levels and releases the feel good
chemical dopamine in the brain. When dopamine is released mood
elevation typically occurs, which ensures that you will likely eat
again. When I eat something that tastes good, it is almost like my
brain feels happy. When I eat something that tastes terrible, it is
almost like I am not eating food at all. When I eat something that
gives me a natural high, I know it because my eyes begin to tear up,
I constantly talk about how great the food is, and sometimes I even

take pictures of the food. My friends think it is a little weird, but what do they know? To them, Papa John's is great pizza.

I really did not appreciate a lot of good food until I began cooking. I read recently that one of the best ways to get a child to eat different foods is to invite him into the kitchen so that he can become part of the cooking process. Personally, I was in college when I was struck by the cooking bug. The cafeteria at my school was a step above awful. The only thing it had going for it was that it was "all you can eat." To me the food was so horrible they should have put up a sign that read, "All you should eat," with tiny portions on a plate. I finally got fed up in my junior year when it became depressing for me to go the cafeteria. I begged my mother to send me the money that she would have sent the food services people for my meal plan. With that money, I began to eat like a king. Guys would stop by my room and ask me how they could get on my meal plan. The only downside was that during the week I started eating alone more often. I quickly learned that a big part of the eating natural high is breaking bread with good friends and family.

When I was in graduate school I finally had an apartment – and more importantly a kitchen – of my own. Each day I would work hard in the biology lab (often getting frustrated that my experiments were not working) and each night I returned home to watch Molto Mario on the Food Network make dinner. It was a sad existence until it dawned on me that I should start to make some of the dishes I was seeing on television. The only problem was that I was broke. Then one night I watched him make gnocchi with pesto. Gnocchi is potato pasta, which combines two things I love, potatoes and pasta. When I realized that all it took to make the pasta was two potatoes, eggs and flour, I was blown away. I thought, "Even I can do that!" Several failed attempts later I made some pretty good looking gnocchi. What about the sauce? Well, I cheated at first and just bought some pesto sauce. When I tossed the whole thing together I almost fell off my borrowed couch. I was eating a gourmet meal that would cost me over $20 in a restaurant. Soon my eyes welled up and I was taking pictures like a fool.

PF Chang's
Not to brag, but in January of 2007 I spent a week speaking in North Vernon, Indiana. While at the local Wal-Mart, I told the checkout clerk that I was in the area for the week and she said, "You're stuck here all week? I'm so sorry!" I looked at her and said, "You're sorry? You live here." Honestly, it is a very nice place, but being away for a week in the dead of winter makes many places seem dull. On my way back to the hotel, I scanned the radio stations desperately seeking entertainment. As I pulled into the parking lot, I settled on a station where I heard a caller telling a story about the biggest surprise of her life. This is basically what she said:

"I was dog sitting for my friends who had this really big, really old dog. On the second night, the dog fell asleep and never woke up! I was panicked, so I called the vet. He calmed me by saying, 'Don't worry. He was old, just bring him over tomorrow.' Weighing as much as the dog, I had no idea how to get it to the vet. So I looked around their house and found a large suitcase…"

At this point of the story, I was about to leave my car. It wasn't that funny, but it sounded interesting and hey, I was stuck in Indiana.

"…Once I got the dog in the suitcase I realized that I did not have access to a car nor would a cab be an option. There was no way I was going to have a cab driver catch me with this thing. So I set off for the subway. The wheels on the suitcase made the trip very easy. I took the escalator down to my train, got off at the stop and was devastated to learn that the escalator was out! I began pulling the suitcase up the stairs and must have looked ridiculous, because a man offered his help. He looked a little sketchy, but I needed the help. As he pulled the suitcase up the stair, he asked, 'What's in this thing?' I told him it was computer equipment and as he reached the top of the stairs, I reached for my wallet to give him a tip. Just then he turned and sprinted down the street with the suitcase!"

At that point, I had a huge belly laugh because I did not see it coming. I couldn't imagine what would be funnier – the reaction of her friends when she explained that their dog is not only dead, but stolen, or the look on the robber's face when he opened the suitcase. For me, it was just one of those great moments in life when laughter lifted my spirits and made me forget where I was and what I was doing. Suddenly, Indiana in the freezing cold did not seem so bad. In fact, I was so motivated by the good feelings that I decided to treat myself to a decent meal. In Indiana that means an hour drive to a PF Chang's, but it was totally worth it. The entire evening boosted my mood – it all began with the natural high of laughter, and ended with the natural high of eating great food. Well, great food for Indiana.

Inspirational Pizza

"I ate a pizza once that was so good it made me cry. There is nothing creepier than a grown man eating and weeping."
- Matt Bellace

The simplest way to achieve a food natural high is to eat the simplest of all foods – pizza. I have always loved it, but until college I never realized that not all pizza is created equally. When I arrived on campus my first week, I asked where to go for the best pizza. One of the students suggested Vennari's, a popular place decorated with photos from all the past and present students who had eaten there. I was two bites into my first Vennari's slice when it hit me, "Oh no, if this is the best pizza around I am in trouble." Panic set in as I realized that fall break was more than two months away and my only other pizza option was cafeteria pizza. I broke out in a cold sweat as I examined the happy faces on the wall. "Liars," I thought. They must have been from Ohio or something.

Sacrifice is one of the great buildups to a natural high. If you go without something and you know it, the return to it is even sweeter. When I returned home over break, I went out with some friends to get some of the best thin crust pizza in New Jersey. The place is called Star Tavern in Orange. The restaurant has such a great Jersey neighborhood vibe going on inside. The first time I had eaten there was in high school with my American Legion baseball team. The pizza was so good that I remember saying, "Wow, I now know why the Romans used to eat, throw up, and eat more." That quote is not meant to make light of people struggling with bulimia, I was just sad to be full.

Exercise: The Pizza Bucket List

Below are my top five favorite pizza places in the country. I wish for you the means to visit most – if not all – of these wonderful places before you die. The great thing about pizza is that it's always affordable and when it is done right it's as good as any gourmet meal.

Keste', 271 Bleeker St., New York, NY 10003, (212) 477-9950
This Greenwich Village pizza spot is arguably the best pizza in New York City. The owner trained in Naples, Italy and is so obsessed with making pizza the right way he flew in an expert pizza oven builder from Italy to make the oven. This Neopolitan pizza may cost a little more, but it is completely worth it. Also, if the tiny place is packed and you have to wait to get in – check out the famous Murray's Cheese down the block.

Di Fara's Pizza, 1424 Ave. J, at E. 15th St., Brooklyn, NY 11230, (718) 258-1367
It is a pain to drive to Brooklyn and an even bigger pain to stand on line for up to three hours for this amazing pizza, but after one bite you'll forget the wait. Every pie in this throwback of a pizza joint is made by the 70-something Dominic De Marco. Watching him work is one of the highlights of the entire experience – that, and seeing New Yorkers stand on line for three hours and not complain. The décor in this place is not worthy of date night, so I recommend going with friends.

Geno's East, Various Locations, Chicago, IL (www.genoseast.com)
The busiest speaking day in the history of my speaking career – five programs in one day all around the Chicago suburbs – was capped off

by a trip to Geno's East in downtown Chicago. This pizza institution has been serving up some of the finest deep dish in the country since 1966. I am usually a purist when it comes to pizza, preferring the thin crust style from Naples, Italy. But if you're in the Midwest, do as the Midwesterners do and get into some deep dish. Be prepared to wait like 45 minutes for your pie, though. It takes a long time to make a good dish, but it is worth the wait.

Two Amy's Pizza, 3715 Macomb St. NW, Washington, DC 20016, (202) 885-5700

I was recently speaking at The Sidwell Friends School in D.C. The school is probably best known for two things – the Obama girls and being down the block from 2 Amy's. The style of pizza at 2 Amy's is thin crust Neapolitan, which means it is only cooked in a wood-burning oven. It felt like I was back in Italy enjoying a lunchtime meal. My favorite is the Margherita Pizza – simply tomato, Buffalo mozzarella and basil. I also loved the laid back atmosphere and great appetizers.

Motorino, 349 12th Street - East Village, b/n 1st/2nd Avenues, New York, NY (212) 777-2644

Owner Mathieu Palombino bought the storefront and wood burning oven of the famous Una Pizza Napoletana after it suddenly closed in 2009. My wife and I had a date night there recently and I was skeptical it could live up to its puritanical predecessor. However, after sampling the bread and heavenly Margherita Pizza I became a believer. Every pie uses buffalo mozzarella and imported San Marzano tomatoes. Afterwards, we were lucky to meet Mathieu. His passion for creating great pizza was evident as he explained his process of experimenting with "25 different doughs" during the past year. If you eat there, do yourself a favor and have dessert around the corner at the Momofuku Milk Bar - 207 Second Ave. at the corner of 13th and Second. I recommend the Cereal Milk™ Soft Serve Ice Cream.

Honorable Mentions: *Sally's APizza* (New Haven, CT), *Pizzeria Bianco* (Phoeniz, AZ), *Star Tavern* (Orange, NJ)

Brain Facts: Eating and the Brain

In recent years, obesity researchers have been exploring the neurological pathways involved in eating and overeating. The mesolimbic brain pathway is a complex neural network that regulates many emotional and motivational processes involved in reward. Eating is an inherently rewarding process. The process of eating often begins with feelings of hunger, which at times can be an uncomfortable feeling. The hungrier you get, the more you want to eat. Once you have eaten, the discomfort decreases while feelings of satiation and pleasure increase. Dopamine is the neurochemical that is believed to be involved in the motivation for a reward or the "wanting" part of a food reward. The "liking" part of a food reward is believed to be mediated by different neurochemicals known as opiates.[1] A recent study showed that increasing opiates in the brain of an animal that has already eaten can actually cause it to eat more than an animal that is just food-deprived.[2]

Taking in different nutrients – like fats and sugars – normally produces effects on the brain and behavior. I find it fascinating that the same neural pathway is used when someone eats sugars and fats as when someone takes a drug of abuse. When fats and sugars are consumed in excess, this releases an excessive amount of dopamine, similar to the process involved when someone abuses cocaine or amphetamines.[3] Laboratory studies have shown that rats will binge on sugar and fat separately, but that the combination of sweet and fat together produces the most pronounced binges. For example, rats will consume almost 60% of their daily calorie intake within a 2 hr binge when given ample access to a combination of sweets and fats.[4] These results are consistent with my personal experience. I have finished big meals – I mean huge meals where I am completely full – and somehow reading food words makes me want more. It's like I'm thinking, "You know I'm disgustingly bloated and full right now, but reading this word 'tiramisu' makes me want to eat more."

Learning How to Eat: Slow Food

> *"I guess all food is slow food.*
> *If it had been fast, it wouldn't be food."*
> -Matt Bellace

During a trip to Italy in 2007, my wife and I had quite an eating adventure. We were staying in the Tuscany region of Italy and each day we would travel to these small hill towns, walk around and eat the most incredible food you could imagine. I ate a Tuscan bread soup called Ribollita that gave me the symptoms of an eating natural high – watering eyes, big smiles, and wild statements like, "This is the best soup on earth!" I ordered Ribollita every time I saw it on a menu in Tuscany and was never disappointed. Inevitably, at some point after the meal we would walk around town and come across a table with a sign that read, "Slow Food Movement." Italians are not exactly known for eating quickly, so that concept seemed kind of funny to us. Perhaps they thought three hour dinners were not long enough.

It turns out that the Slow Food movement had finally hit its tipping point and was receiving international attention with a simple concept. Everyone has a fundamental right to eat good, clean food. The movement is founded upon the strong connections between the plate and our planet. They believe that eating well should not harm the environment, animal welfare, or our health. At the same time, proponents of this movement believe that food producers should receive fair compensation for their work. The movement actually began in Northern Italy back in 1986. The founding father of the Slow Food Movement, Italian Carlo Petrini, recognized that the industrialization of food was standardizing taste and leading to the annihilation of thousands of food varieties and flavors. He wanted to reach out to consumers and demonstrate to them that they have choices over fast food and supermarket homogenization. He rallied his friends and his community, and began to speak out at every available opportunity about the effects of a fast culture. With the preservation of taste a main priority, he sought to support and protect small growers and artisanal producers, support and protect the physical environment, and promote biodiversity. Today, the organization that Petrini and his colleagues founded is active in over 100 countries and has a worldwide membership of over 80,000 people.

An understanding of the Slow Food movement is vital to a chapter on healthy eating natural highs. The culture of fast food and supermarkets has disconnected people from the origins of their food. For example, when you go to a fast food place and order some nugget of chicken, deep fried and dipped in sauce, you are completely removed from any part of the food processing. You don't see the chicken ahead of time. You barely even see it while you are eating it. Unless you bite the nugget in half and make a point to look at it before you dip, how do you know if it is white or green? Presumably, the chicken nugget is safe to eat. But is it good to eat?

The "Brain Facts" section of this chapter discusses the connection between foods high in fat and sugar and addiction to food. Fast food provides us with a perfect example of an unhealthy natural high. The food is loaded with sugar and fat, which tastes great in the moment and leaves you wanting more. But eating is a natural high that should ideally be a healthy natural high. The only way to achieve this is to eat a balanced diet that consists of more natural foods, and natural foods tend not to be processed into high fat, high sugar nuggets.

When I was a kid I loved to eat Easy Cheese and anything with ketchup. To me there were two food groups – ketchup, and all things that you ate with ketchup. If that kid eating tons of ketchup could grow up to appreciate natural foods, then anyone can. You may not love Italian food – perhaps you prefer Thai or Southwestern cooking. It really does not matter what type of cuisine you like, the Slow Food movement is more about locally grown meats and vegetables that represent the true flavors of food. In fact, if you travel to the country of origin of your favorite foods you will find that the best restaurants tend to serve foods made from the freshest ingredients.

One of the best areas of the country to experience the Slow Food Movement is in California. In fact, the state looks so much like Italy that sometimes I mess it up in my brain and refer to our trips to California as our trips to Italy! I feel like in California, you can walk into almost any food establishment and get fresher, less processed food than you can anywhere else in the country. One of the reasons that California has developed into a Slow Food capital of the United States is the influence of Alice Waters. If Carlo Patrini is the father of the Slow Food Movement, then Alice Waters is the mother. Thirty seven years ago she started a restaurant in Berkeley, CA called Chez Panisse. But it wasn't just the cooking that made her famous – it was the ingredients. She was one of the first to serve antibiotic and hormone free meats and insisted on fresh, organic, locally-grown fruits and vegetables.

The good news for many people is that the organic movement has taken over our country. There are many regions that have embraced Slow Foods. In the Berkshire Mountains of Western Massachusetts, you can find ample locally grown pork and cheese products. If you are one of the millions of people who commute to the Jersey Shore or the Hamptons in the summer, there are literally dozens of local farmers who sell their locally grown fruits and vegetables along the side of the road. Even Wal-Mart sells organic produce, which means if you live two hours east of Pittsburgh – in like Johnstown, PA or something – you can still eat organic. Not that I ever had to do that on October 23, 2007.

Exercise: Pick up a Zagat Guide and highlight the restaurants that serve your favorite cuisine. Select two or three with the highest food ratings that are still in your price range, and try them out. Chances are you will find that the food is fresher and better tasting than the fast food versions. For more information about the Slow Food Movement, check out www.slowfood.com. If you live in New York City and want to find the nearest farmers market, visit www.cenyc.org/greenmarket.

Learning How to Eat: Your Own Cooking

"Eating in Italy is like a dream. I almost forgot I was American
until the tour bus from New Jersey arrived. In walked Johnny Guappo
and these Goodfellas wannabes yelling, 'This place sucks!
No mozzarella sticks? We're goin' back to Bayonne.'"
-Matt Bellace

Let's say you live in Tigerton, Wisconsin. The town is two hours from that booming metropolis of a city called Green Bay and three hours from the only real civilization around in Minneapolis. Anyone who lives in these areas knows that good, healthy food is hard to find. In Tigerton, I went out to the only restaurant in town. It was attached to a gas station and their most popular item was fried cheese curds. This appetizer is basically cheddar cheese curds (a.k.a., uncooked cheddar), dipped in batter and fried. The basket was dripping with so much oil you would swear they poured it on themselves. The best part was when the waitress handed me a bottle of ranch dressing and said, "You can't have these without ranch dressing." Yeah, it must help grease the angioplasty rod so the heart surgeons can clean out my carotid artery.

I lived in a poor food town for almost six years and when I couldn't travel, I had the good stuff brought to me. In this age of the internet and FedEx, amazing eats are just a few clicks away. The best place to start to learn how to cook is by watching authentic cooking shows. I am not talking about Rachael Ray or that over-enunciating Giatta DeLaurentis. I mean television chefs who can really cook. For the Italian food fan, that means Lidia Bastianich of the PBS show "Lidia's Italy" or Mario Batalli of Fine Living Network's "Molto Mario." There are also a slew of great demos on YouTube of cooks making dishes that will give you the eating natural high.

Once you have the ingredients you need and a kitchen in which to cook them, my advice is to start simple. Pick out one dish that you think would be cool to make at home, like pizza or soup. Focus all of your energy on one dish and keep trying it until you perfect it. It's important to remember that the ingredients are everything for great dishes. If you cannot find a particular ingredient in your local supermarket, you may need to try a specialty shop or mail order. I would not start with something that requires expensive ingredients. You don't want to be paying back a failed white truffle dish forever.

If you have a real interest in cooking, perhaps you can find a cooking class that will teach you the basics. Cooking always got a bad rap in grade school among my friends. They called it 'gay.' That was their favorite word for everything. I always found it ironic that what they thought was not masculine got me more dates in my twenties than all the kickball homeruns I ever made in gym class. In my opinion, there are few things more intimate than breaking bread with friends or a romantic interest. There is just something about giving the gift of good food that feels great.

The Pellegrino Revolution

> *My uncle yelled at me, 'You don't drink wine?*
> *How do you eat your food?'*
> *'Um, I chew it?'*
> *-Matt Bellace*

I am Italian American and I do not drink wine. I have spent time on vineyards, tasted Chiantis and Pinot Grigios, and learned about the process of producing wines, but the taste of wine does nothing for me. I respect the rights of any adult to enjoy wine or any alcohol in moderation, but it is not for me. As a high school student I didn't drink because I didn't want to get into trouble. In college I was a social activist making a point. Now, despite knowing that I can drink, I decide not to because of the taste.

In people over age 21, "moderate drinking" is defined as one or two drinks per day. Consuming more than this increases your risk of developing many types of cancers and dementia.[5,6] My maternal grandmother suffered from Alzheimer's dementia and I know it is not something I want more of in my life. Interestingly, many people drink to excess during natural high events, like meals, comedy shows or sporting events. In fact, there are times when the chemical high overwhelms the natural high and people's behavior changes for the worst. I remember a comedy show when a woman – who appeared to be very intoxicated – thought that one of my jokes was her personal invitation to join me on stage. She actually made her way onto the stage and grabbed for the microphone just before her horrified boyfriend pulled her off stage. It was such a bizarre moment that as they left the club during my set, I shouted, "Don't leave, you're the funniest thing that will happen here all night!"

There are many drinks that I find go well with a great meal. Sparkling water is one of my favorites. There is a restaurant in Sausalito, CA called Poggio that creates its own sparkling water from the restaurant's well. If sparkling water is not your thing, there has been an explosion of specialty iced teas, lemonades, and vitamin drinks that not only taste great, but are often good for you. I love green iced tea with honey – all brands. I have never seen a drink that is literally so good that I don't mind what brand it is. In recent years, there has been a big movement in schools away from offering sodas and other sugary drinks in an effort to combat obesity. I think it is great for schools to model healthier habits. I know so many people who are convinced that they could never like water, but I find that when I follow up a good workout with a great meal, water is the first thing on my mind.

Exercise: Make an effort to try healthier beverage options. For example, if you consume three cans of soda per day, try drinking only one with dinner. If you live on beverages like diet soda, perhaps try something more natural like hot or iced tea with honey. If you have doubts that you will enjoy it, do an experiment. Give it two weeks and see if the change is different than you anticipated.

Summary

Eating when you are hungry or drinking when you are thirsty always feels good. In fact, I look forward to the summer because I love that sensation of sweating, getting really thirsty, and then quenching that thirst with a tall, cold glass of water. The natural high of eating comes from the increase in blood sugar in the body and the release of dopamine in the reward centers of the brain. Experiencing eating natural highs, in my opinion, is also about being open-minded to trying new foods, drinks and cooking techniques. In the end, good food is always better when shared with good friends.

CHAPTER FIVE

Unhealthy Natural Highs

"I'M 38 YEARS OLD AND OFFICIALLY
IN THE SECOND HALF OF LIFE.
I DON'T LIKE THE SECOND HALF,
BECAUSE I KNOW HOW IT ENDS – I LOSE."
- DAN NATURMAN

A discussion of natural highs would be incomplete without a chapter about unhealthy natural highs. These highs are obtained without the use of alcohol or other drugs, but can still be physically and mentally harmful. One unhealthy natural high, known as the "choking game," can cause brain damage after just one exposure. The truth is just about any natural high activity can be harmful if it is done to excess. For example, running too much can make you dangerously thin and/or excessively preoccupied with exercise. Eating too much can make you morbidly obese, and loving someone too much… well, that can make you a stalker. Of course, it wasn't stalking when Enrique Iglesias sang, "You can run, you can hide, but you can't escape my love." I said that to a girl once. Apparently that is enough for a restraining order.

This chapter provides a brief overview of the most common unhealthy natural highs. It includes some obvious unhealthy natural highs, such as problem gambling, overeating, excessive exercise, and high risk sexual behavior. In addition, it also describes some not-so-obvious ones such as the "choking game," cutting, video game/internet addiction, and adrenaline junkies.

Problem Gambling

"I'm told it costs $30,000 to treat a gambling addiction.
How much you want to bet it doesn't work?"
-Matt Bellace

When I was in high school, there were a bunch of guys who started playing a game called "flipping." I don't even remember it well, but I know that it involved throwing pennies against a wall to see who could land the closest to the wall without touching it. It seemed totally random, but a couple of guys I know were completely into it. They would flip every weekend and during lunch if they could find a spot. I tried it, but never stayed for long because I hated losing money. I guess I'm genetically predisposed to cheapness because the idea of giving away your money and getting nothing for it was painful. However, one of the guys was so into flipping that he began stealing money from his job at 7-Eleven to pay for his gambling. When he got caught, he was fired from the job, and got into trouble with the police. He was also grounded by his parents, suspended from school, and got kicked off the football team. Other than that he was fine. Looking back at it I'm glad I felt the pain of losing my own money rather than stealing someone else's.

Pathological gambling, or "problem gambling," is considered by psychologists to be an impulse control disorder. One of the main features of impulse control disorders is the failure to resist an impulse or temptation to perform an act that is harmful to the person or others. Gambling becomes a harmful high once the gambler begins taking greater and greater risks. If someone is willing to lose large sums of money and risk their job and/or relationships just in order to gamble then they have a problem. Gambling is also illegal in most states for people under the age of 18, which makes it instantly illegal for young people. On the one hand making it illegal probably intensifies the high experience, but doing it instantly makes it a high risk behavior.

If you suspect that someone may have a problem with gambling, ask yourself the following questions: Is the person preoccupied with gambling or do they have a need to gamble with increasingly larger amounts of money? Has the person tried to cut back (unsuccessfully) or do they become restless or irritable when trying to stop? Is gambling a way for them to escape from their problems? In addition, does the person lie, commit illegal acts, and/or risk significant relationships all to keep their gambling habit going? Finally, does the person rely on others to provide them with money to relieve desperate financial situations caused by gambling? If you're answering "yes" to several of these questions, it is time to encourage the person to seek professional help.

In recent years there has been a dramatic increase in the availability of gambling options in the United States. Internet gambling has basically turned the home computer into a slot machine. For a problem gambler, the internet is available around the clock and can be like a loaded gun. Problem gambling is believed to affect 1-2% of the U.S. population. A random telephone survey that was recently conducted with 2,274 U.S. residents 14-21 years old revealed that 68% of respondents had gambled in the past year and 11% gambled at a frequency of twice per week.[1] These young people could be in training to become the problem gamblers of tomorrow.

The good news is that if you need to seek help for yourself, a friend or loved one, there is hope. There are two common forms of treatment for problem gamblers – Gamblers Anonymous (GA) and Cognitive Behavioral Therapy (CBT). GA (www.gamblersanonymous.org) exists as more of a support group for those with gambling addictions. Very little research has examined the relative efficacy of GA programs. Despite this, GA is a self-help treatment that is free of charge, and is often the only treatment option available in many communities. GA meetings can be found in most residential treatment programs and community centers. In contrast, CBT is a professional form of treatment conducted by a clinical psychologist in both individual and group settings. CBT focuses on the thoughts, behaviors, and feelings that trigger and maintain the behaviors associated with gambling. To find a CBT trained psychologist, you can visit www.aabt.org. One recent study found that there were no significant differences in treatment success when comparing CBT and GA.[2] Overall, participants who attended more sessions – regardless of whether it was part of a GA or CBT program – tended to achieve better outcomes than those who did not undergo any intervention for their problematic behaviors. In light of the increasing prevalence of problem gambling, more research is clearly needed in order to determine the most effective treatment for those struggling with this often debilitating disorder.

Brain Facts: Problem Gambling and Dopamine
The brain chemical dopamine plays a major role in the reward system of both humans and animals. Any behavior that makes you feel good and makes you want to engage in the behavior again likely involves dopamine. When someone goes to a casino and wins, they will experience positive feelings. The next time that person thinks about gambling, they are more likely to do it since the behavior has been reinforced by the positive feelings of winning money.

In neuroscience, we often learn about the way healthy brains work by looking at brains that are diseased. For example, recent studies have shown that patients with Parkinson Disease – a degenerative disease of the brain that reduces dopamine levels and impairs muscle functioning – are also more likely to develop gambling problems.[3] The simple conclusion might be that these patients are "giving up on life" and "going for broke" at the casinos. However, it turns out that there is actually a connection between Parkinson's, gambling, and a drug used to treat the disease. One type of drug used to treat Parkinson's is called a dopamine agonist. This is basically a class of drugs that mimics the effect of dopamine in the brain and helps alleviate some of the symptoms of the disease. However, the administration of a dopamine agonist has been shown in recent studies to cause patients in their 50's and 60's with no prior history of gambling problems to start gambling. These patients report that they engage in high risk gambling – occasionally losing thousands of dollars – and have no real explanation for why they started. Interestingly, when the dopamine agonist is reduced the gambling problem subsides. The authors do not know exactly why the medication is influencing a gambling behavior, but let's hope the casinos do not found out!

Overeating

> *"I was just in Las Vegas and I lost a lot of money.*
> *But I get 'em back at the buffet – $9.95 all you can eat, we'll see who*
> *wins this hand. I got to the prime rib table and said, 'Hit Me.'"*
> *-John Pinette*

The natural high of eating has an ugly cousin called overeating. It can come in many forms, such as binge eating, grazing, or simply eating too much in any one sitting. Binge eating is defined as eating, within two hours or less (for some it takes only ten minutes), what most people would consider to be a large amount of food, while experiencing a sense of loss of control. This loss of control is typically described as feeling as though it is difficult to stop eating, and/or to control what or how much you are eating. Those who have engaged in overeating and/or binge eating for many years are often referred to as obese, morbidly obese, or even "super obese." The latter term makes it sound like you are some sort of eating super hero. The problem is that overeating has become an epidemic in our country as many individuals have difficulty maintaining reasonable portion control. Overeating costs people money, quality of life, and health. Scientists believe that there are similarities between overeating and drug addiction. In fact, the neurochemical dopamine has been suggested to have a common role in drug abuse and obesity.[4]

According to the Centers for Disease Control and Prevention, 16 percent of children (over 9 million) 6-19 years old are overweight or obese – a number that has tripled since 1980. In addition to the 16 percent of children and teens who were overweight in 1999-2002, another 15 percent were considered at risk of becoming overweight. Overweight adolescents have a 70 percent chance of becoming overweight or obese adults. This risk increases to 80 percent if one or more parents of an individual is overweight or obese.[5]

This alarming rate of obesity is a particular problem because of its implications for the health of Americans. Obesity increases the risk of many diseases and health conditions, including:

- Coronary Heart Disease
- Type 2 Diabetes
- Cancers (Endometrial, Breast, and Colon)
- Hypertension (i.e., high blood pressure)
- Dyslipidemia
  (e.g., high total cholesterol or high levels of triglycerides)
- Stroke
- Liver and Gallbladder Disease
- Sleep Apnea and other respiratory problems
- Osteoarthritis
  (i.e., degeneration of cartilage and its underlying bone)
- Gynecological problems (e.g., abnormal menses, infertility)

In a study that looked at the economic impact of childhood obesity from 2002-2005, obese children required $194 more in annual outpatient doctor visit expenditures, $114 more in annual prescription drug expenditures, and $12 more in annual emergency room expenditures compared to children of average weight.[6] When these data are extrapolated to all the children in the nation, children with an elevated BMI would be associated with $14.1 billion in additional prescription drug, emergency room, and outpatient visit costs annually. I never realized obesity was such a big profit maker for hospitals. I'm thinking if these children suddenly lost weight the government would have to bail out more than just McDonald's.

Unfortunately, too many people choose to treat their problem of overeating with another extreme measure – fad dieting. A diet is flawed from the start because it typically involves making changes to your eating habits that are not sustainable over the long term. A recent study published in the New England Journal of Medicine looked at the outcomes of dieters using various different fad diets, such as Atkins or The Zone Diet.[7] Each diet touted its own combination of fat-to-carbohydrate intake ratios. The results suggested that reduced calorie diets, regardless of what types of nutrients they emphasize, all result in clinically significant weight-loss. In the end, the ratio of calories you take in to calories you burn in a given day is the most important factor that determines whether an individual will lose weight over time. Of course, you should always speak to your doctor before beginning any weight loss program.

The most tragic aspect of obesity is the loss of quality of life. A friend of mine was morbidly obese for most of his life. From a natural highs perspective, it was hard – even impossible – for him to enjoy active natural highs like running, biking, or surfing. In fact, even walking – especially in warm weather – was such a nuisance for him because he would sweat so much. Eventually he needed gastric bypass surgery to save his life because for him, diet and exercise were not enough. Since the surgery, he has lost a considerable amount of weight and increased his activity level, which is quite admirable. However, his successful surgery was far from easy. He is now faced with a skin reduction surgery to tighten all the loose skin. He also experiences a constant struggle not to overeat – which is easy to do when your stomach is a quarter of its original size! In addition, this surgery itself unfortunately did not teach my friend what it means to consume moderate portions of appropriate foods.

He and I had dinner together a few weeks ago at a great pizza place near his home. He was over two years post-surgery and doing well. At the meal, he ate what was a normal amount for me, but it was a little too much for him, and on the way home had some gastrointestinal distress. I normally would not kid about someone's medical condition, but he has such a great sense of humor about his diarrhea that I had to share. We were driving through the city streets at the time when he alerted me to his situation. I tried to lighten the mood and asked him, "How far along are you?" As someone with irritable bowel syndrome, I classify my situation based on the Defcon System. Defcon 5 would indicate a normal, peaceful bowel situation. Defcon 4 would indicate a normal, but heightened alert bowel – the typical post-meal grumbling. Defcon 3 is a state of increased readiness to evacuate. In my mind you've got fifteen to twenty minutes tops until detonation. Defcon 2 requires immediate action towards the proper facilities. Time is of the essence and there is little room for error. When Defcon 1 is reached, you had better be in on the throne or near a pizza box. It is beyond the point of no return. Well, he was at Defcon 3 and we were about thirty minutes from home. I pleaded with him, "Stop off at a Starbucks or Dunkin' Donuts. Why stress?" He looked at me and said, "No, I have a thing about public bathrooms." As he slipped closer to Defcon 2, I could see the sweat beading on his forehead. As we passed a California Pizza Kitchen, I screamed out, "Just go in. Don't be a hero!" We both burst out laughing, which was not helpful. He was able to make it home in time, but it must be tough to live a life in fear of being too far from a decent bathroom.

Excessive Exercising

"My first time working out I had no idea what I was doing.
This guy at the gym asked, 'So, what are you working out?'
I said, 'Childhood issues? Is there a machine for that?'"
- Ted Alexandro

Exercise – like most natural highs – can be abused when it is done to excess. How is "excessive" defined? Well, research psychologists use four criteria: 1) exercising more than 2 hours per day and having distress if unable to exercise, 2) exercise causes significant interference with important activities, 3) frequent exercise at inappropriate times and places and little or no attempt to suppress the behavior, and/or 4) exercising despite more serious injury, illness or medical complications. Excessive exercise tends to be associated with eating disorders – like anorexia nervosa or bulimia nervosa – which are among the deadliest of the psychiatric conditions.[8]

My wife Dara Bellace, PhD is a clinical psychologist who specializes in the treatment of eating disorders. Based on what I've learned from her, I am aware that a comprehensive discussion of eating disorders could fill this entire book and then some. For the purposes of our discussion, it is important to realize the difference between normal exercise and over-exercise. Exercise can be a terrific way to strengthen muscles, improve circulation, and elevate mood, but when it is used solely to purge the body of excess calories or to compensate for eating certain foods it is a problem. Excessive exercise is most common among the purging subtype of anorexia nervosa.[9] However, individuals who are of a normal weight or even somewhat overweight can also engage in this problematic behavior. Over-exercising may go unnoticed at first, but after a few months – as the person loses more and more weight – they begin to look unhealthy. A malnourished person can have pale skin, thin and brittle hair and a sunken look to their face. They may try to hide their thinness with oversized shirts or big glasses. You may notice unusual things like they always seem to be at the gym and their workouts may consist of significant amounts of time spent on cardio equipment (e.g., the treadmill or elliptical machine). They may also go through an amazing amount of sneakers.

A 1999 study reported that more than half of 5th through 12th grade girls were unhappy with their body weight and shape, and that the unhappiness was strongly related to dieting to lose weight and exercising to lose weight.[10] Glamour magazines, television and the internet often portray images of young women who look perfect and almost impossibly thin. These images are often altered and airbrushed to remove blemishes and body fat, but the viewer is not aware of this. The implicit message to young women is if you do not look like these images then you are not attractive. This is incredibly unfortunate because many of these young women and some young men will begin dieting and exercising to extremes in an effort to achieve a look that is not even realistic.

If you know someone who has a problem with over-exercising or someone you think may have an eating disorder, there is help available. There are treatment centers that specialize in diagnosing and treating individuals with eating disorders. A good treatment center for eating disorders tends to take a multidisciplinary approach, with psychiatrists, psychologists, nutritionists and other medical professionals on staff. Ideally, the treatment facility should consist of specialized inpatient and outpatient services so that each phase of an individual's treatment can be provided in a comprehensive manner. Many academic medical centers tend to provide this level of specialized, responsible care for individuals struggling with eating disorders. In addition to providing state-of-the-art care, they are often conducting treatment studies which provide treatment free of charge if you qualify. For more information, please visit www.edreferral.com.

High-Risk Sexual Behavior

> *"A girl called me up and said,*
> *'Rodney, come on over – there's nobody home.'*
> *I went over – nobody was home."*
> *-Rodney Dangerfield*

Sex is the purest form of a natural high. The brain rewards itself for having sex by releasing feel good neurotransmitters. Scientists believe that the evolutionary reason sex feels good is to increase the chances that humans will continue to seek it out to reproduce and keep the species going. The chapter on "Loving" focuses on the natural high of not just sex, but love. As simple as the natural high of sex may be, the act of really loving someone and maintaining a relationship is anything but simple. This is obvious in the number of stories on the news about young people who thought they were being flirtatious by sexting (i.e. sending nude pictures of themselves to someone) and ended up in trouble or worse, completely embarrassed. It is not any easier for older people either. Each week we see a new celebrity or politician get busted for an extramarital affair, putting the natural high of sex over the natural high of loving their long term partner. Of course, the frequency of commercials for male erectile dysfunction or articles about low female sexual desire make you wonder how older people even have the desire for one relationship, let alone more. But when it comes to high-risk sexual behavior, the threat is more than just your reputation or relationships, it can be physically and mentally harmful.

The New York City Department of Health and Mental Hygiene announced in June 2008 that more than one-fourth of adult New Yorkers are infected with the sexually transmitted disease Herpes Simplex Virus 2 – the virus that causes Genital Herpes. This prevalence is higher than the 19 percent national average and concerning – not just because it is nasty – but because it facilitates the spread of the H.I.V. virus. Genital Herpes is sexually transmitted and its symptoms include genital ulcers or sores and even infections of the brain. NYC's rates of Gonorrhea, Chlamydia, and infectious Syphilis are also above the national average.

The New Yorkers that contracted sexually transmitted diseases may not have been aware that they were participating in high-risk sexual behavior when they contracted their disease. You don't have to be paying a prostitute for sex or having unprotected sex with a stranger to be engaging in high-risk sexual activity. There are many forms of high-risk sexual activity that involve things you may not have previously considered. For example, having sex with someone who is emotionally abusive to you is a high-risk sexual behavior because it may cause psychological pain. The pain may not even come during the act, but rather later when you learn they were cheating on you or spreading rumors about you. Having sex while under the influence of alcohol and other drugs can increase a person's risk taking behavior.

As a student at Bucknell University, I was a member of a fraternity. I was only active for two years, but it was an eventful time in my development. One night, our fraternity – Phi Kappa Psi – had a mixer with their favorite sorority. One of our pledges proceeded to get drunk and "hook-up" with one of the similarly drunk sorority sisters. This was so commonplace at the time that very few people even noticed that night. Apparently, the two ended up back in the dorm in either his or her room and they had sex. The next morning, the young woman pressed charges claiming that she had been passed out and did not consent to having sex. The young man denied this and claimed that the sex was consensual. The case was brought up in both the local court and within the campus judicial system. The local court threw the case out because both parties admitted to being so drunk they could not remember many details of the evening. The Bucknell campus judicial system was not so rigid, however. They ruled in favor of the young lady and expelled our pledge. The young woman later found out that she was pregnant. To her credit, I believe she continued on at school, had the baby and put it up for adoption. I do not know what happened to our pledge. He left school and I have never heard from him again.

The "Choking Game"

> *"I read that each year people drive their cars into lakes and*
> *off cliffs because their GPS system told them to.*
> *Honestly, I'm ok with it – we don't need everyone to have a long life."*
> -Matt Bellace

It is known by many other names – the "pass-out game," "blackout," "flat liner," or "suffocation roulette." The object is the same: choking yourself or having a friend do it for you, passing out, and reviving – waiting for that 10-second high as oxygen rushes back into the brain. The most common age range for kids playing this game is between 9 and 14 years old. However, as I write this very section on the front page of every newspaper in New York City is an article about an adult who went on Craigslist and offered to pay someone to choke him while he masturbated. The pursuit of this unusual high turned violent for some reason and the man was found stabbed to death in his apartment. Obviously, the story highlights several risky behaviors, such as contacting strangers on the internet and meeting up with them, but it also exposes the choking game as more than just school yard activity.

During my clinical psychology internship I treated a 60-year old gentleman for memory loss. He was otherwise in good health, but he was complaining of increased problems with organization, short-term memory loss, and irritability. He reported that his memory was "never good," but had worsened over the past year and it was frustrating for him. There was no history of Alzheimers Disease in his family and no risk factors for vascular dementia. The results of his cognitive testing revealed a profile more similar to someone with a head injury. I had already asked him about a history of concussions, car accidents, or falls and he reported nothing. My supervisor encouraged me to go back and ask more questions about his childhood. As soon as I did, this patient informed me that during middle school he played the choking game more times than he could remember. It would occur during recess or after school when no adult supervision was present. A friend would press him against a wall until he would pass out, and then he would usually wake up within a few seconds. He had never thought that the game could cause brain damage that could impact his memory fifty years later.

In December 2008, an article about my presentations on natural highs appeared in a number of newspapers across the country. As a result, I was contacted by Lyndi Trost, a grandmother who lost her 13-year old grandson Braden in 2005. Braden and his friends had been playing the choking game when it turned deadly. Lyndi noted that there are hundreds of other young victims like her grandson, especially when we consider the number of young people who could sustain brain damage from the activity. She informed me that it is her personal mission to "…make sure that every child beginning in elementary school is educated about the dangers of the choking game." She contacted me in the hopes that I would spread the word about the choking game, having had no idea about the patient I saw or the book I was writing. I kept my promise to Lyndi and feel terrible for her loss.

Brain Facts: Anoxia
It is hard to predict the amount of brain damage that can result from playing the choking game. Brain scanners tend to be better at locating specific areas of brain damage rather than generalized cell death across the brain. In addition, it is hard to know exactly how many other brain insults occur over the course of a person's life, such as those caused by breathing in environmental toxins or a chronic lack of sleep. However, we must remember that we only get one brain in our lifetime and injuries to it are cumulative. Each time a person passes out, brain cells die off. The process is called "anoxia,"

which literally means "without oxygen." Ironically, the area of the brain most affected by anoxia is the memory center of the temporal lobe.[11,12] The memory center is a collection of brain structures that happens to be adjacent to the largest supply of blood entering the brain – the middle cerebral artery. When a person passes out, there is a disruption of blood flow through the middle cerebral artery and cells are immediately impacted. If anoxia lasts longer than a few seconds it can kill someone.

If you are concerned that someone you know might be involved in the pass out game, here are some warning signs: bloodshot eyes, unusual marks on the neck, and belts and ropes found with unusual knots found tied to furniture. For more information about the "Choking Game" go to: www.gaspinfo.com.

Cutting

Highs come in many forms. Some create a sense of happiness and euphoria, while others reduce tension and produce a sense of calm. Chemical highs, like those resulting from the use of Valium or marijuana, have been reported to reduce anxiety and produce an artificial sense of well-being. Natural highs, like a vacation at the ocean or the mountains, can also produce the same sense of well being. However, there is also an unhealthy natural high known as cutting that can create a feeling of reduced tension and calm. On May 6, 2008, The New York Times published these descriptions of cutting in an article by Jane E. Brody:

"I feel relieved and anxious after I cut. The emotional pain slips away into the physical pain. It [cutting] expresses emotional pain or feelings that I'm unable to put into words."

Cutting is not well understood, partly because it is such a secretive activity. Cutting typically occurs in adolescents or young adults, and it tends to be a response to feelings of anger, abuse, or neglect.[13] Experts estimate that this type of self-injury is practiced by 15 percent of the general adolescent population. The individual generally reports feeling extremely tense, anxious, or angry prior to self-mutilation, while a sense of relief, calm, or satisfaction follows. Occasionally these individuals also report feeling guilty or disgusted after cutting themselves.[14] It is important to note that cutting is not a form of attempted suicide. Instead, cutting appears to be a dysfunctional attempt to manage emotions by seeking a sensation that will distract the individual from intense emotions. Unfortunately, these individuals have difficulty coping appropriately with their emotions, thereby resorting to extremely unhealthy and risky behaviors as a maladaptive way to cope (or, really, not cope) with such feelings.

I was reading somewhere that cutting is a socially unacceptable form of self-injury. Then the non-psychologist part of my brain thought, "Are there socially acceptable forms of self-injury?" Of course, how could I forget tongue rings, tattoos, and various other side effects of low self-esteem? That Tom Cruise tattoo seemed like a great idea after Top Gun, but then came Eyes Wide Shut and Oprah's couch and now all you've got is a scar of Tom's head and Hepatitis C.

Cutting is different than a bad tattoo or an earring in your nose. Cutting tends to be a repetitive self-mutilation of the body – typically on the wrists and arms – and is often done with a razor blade. Psychologists believe it may serve to control anger, anxiety, or pain that cannot be expressed verbally or through other healthier means. It is harmful on many levels, but the most damaging is that it prevents an individual from developing healthy coping mechanisms to deal with life's stressors. It is theorized that cutting releases opiate-like endorphins in the brain that result in a high state and subsequent emotional relief.

The treatment for cutting involves a relatively new psychological intervention called Dialectical Behavior Therapy (DBT). DBT is a treatment designed specifically for individuals who engage in self-harm behaviors, as well as those who experience suicidal thoughts and attempts. DBT is a modified form of CBT discussed earlier (see "Problem Gambling" section). Medication for stabilizing mood can also be a part of some treatment plans, as many individuals experience underlying depression or anxiety that may contribute to their behaviors.

Excessive Video Game / Internet Use

"As a kid all I wanted for Christmas was this video game called Atari.
Instead, I got Adari.
He was an exchange student from Pakistan."
-Matt Bellace

In college, there were these computer labs that were open 24 hours a day. I always knew at some point during the semester, I was going to end up there writing a paper at 2 o'clock in the morning. Almost every time I went to this one lab, the same two guys were sitting there. It could be midnight or three in the morning, but there they were. They had that "we've never found a soap we've liked" look about them. By the fourth time I saw them there, I realized that they were not working in the traditional sense. They were doing what my friends called "electronic crack" – playing video games. Their game of choice involved something known as MUD or MUDing. MUD stands for Multi-loser, I'm sorry… Multi-User Domain. Here I am making fun of them. These guys could be running a division of Microsoft right now on their own island in the Pacific. The truth is the concept was actually pretty revolutionary because many players could compete at the same time without having to sit in the same room. The games were text based and helped spawn some of the wildly popular games of today like World of Warcraft and Second Life.

I love video games. I forged many friendships in middle school, high school and college around joysticks. Alright, that was a bad choice of words. Let me start over. Video games are the only thing that can make you angry at a sunny day because you can't see the screen. The moment I beat Mike Tyson in Mike Tyson's Punchout, I was grinning like I was about to get paid for it. Unfortunately, any activity that you do so much it interferes with your relationships, school work, or job can be bad for you. I did not get to know those two guys in the college computer lab. Yet I suspect, at that time, they couldn't help but play games all night and probably neglected their schoolwork. At the very least they neglected their shampoo.

Video games interfered with my own grades at one point during college. I was a sophomore at Bucknell and found myself in a depressing situation. I had gone away to school thinking baseball would be my first priority. I thought that college would be the best four years of my life socially. But less than two years in and I was seeing no playing time on Varsity and my social life was like the movie Groundhog's Day. Every party was the same – drunk people, sticky floors, an aroma of puke and beer, and lots of loud people more interested in drinking than talking.

Video games eventually became a great outlet for me and seemed like a very social experience. There were always guys hanging out willing to play and no parents to tell you to stop. In a way, video games became my coping mechanism when I did not know how to handle a reality that was worse than my expectations. Yet video games are really an altered reality. They exist as an alternative to the real world. The simple act of playing a video game is not unhealthy. It is the repetitive use of the games that can interfere with one's life. If the video games are serving as the only coping mechanism in a person's life, then the video game use only increases once life becomes more stressful. This type of video game use can also become socially isolating, which can often keep someone from seeking the kind of social support that they may really need during difficult times.

In 2007, the American Medical Association decided not to recommend to the American Psychiatric Association that they include Internet Addiction as a formal diagnosis in the 2012 edition of the DSM. Instead, they recommended further research on "video game overuse." In my opinion, there is no question that using video games and the internet can be a lot of fun. Like many other behaviors, when done in moderation, it is a form of a natural high. Yet when treated like a compulsion that interferes with normal functioning in school or at work, it becomes psychologically unhealthy.

Dangerous Risk Taking

"Bear Grylls.
I don't know why they call him that.
I don't think he grills anything - he just eats it raw."
-Matt Bellace

If you are attacked by a grizzly bear and you're not the Man vs. Wild guy, you'll probably have a tremendous surge of the neurotransmitter called epinephrine. Epinephrine is also known as adrenaline and it is involved in the "fight or flight" response. Of course, the Man vs. Wild guy probably stays calm, drinks his own urine, and talks the bear down. Yet when most average human beings are confronted with a Grizzly, they want to jump out of their shoes and run away as fast as they can. Epinephrine increases your attention and can even cause you to perform acts of strength that amaze you. Note: Playing dead is supposed to be better at fending off a bear attack because bears are used to chasing their food.

The term "Adrenaline Junkie" was used in the 1991 movie Point Break and refers to people who engage in dangerous activities just for the adrenaline rush. We tend to think of extreme sports when the term adrenaline rush comes to mind. We can picture some guy getting dropped onto the top of a mountain by a helicopter and skiing down, or even better – surfing a monster wave. These are extreme examples of people who put themselves into harm's way and either have the training to do so, or just a daredevil inside of them that believes they can survive the risk and get out alive. The "junkie" part of the phrase is more about someone who is addicted to the behavior.

There may very well be plenty of extreme sports athletes who are addicted to the danger inherent in their sport – and who end up losing their jobs, money, family or even their lives for their sports. Far more common – and far less interesting – are people who are addicted to drama. These people may love arguments, fights, crises and generally always living under some sort of pressure. This type of activity produces the stress response. Epinephrine is released as a short-term response to stress, along with a chemical called cortisol. Cortisol increases your blood pressure and suppresses your immune system to allow you to focus all of your energy on the problem at hand. That may explain why so many students living under pressure during final exams end up getting sick.

Johnny Drama is one of the main characters in the HBO series Entourage. Despite even the best of circumstances, Drama finds a reason to be anxious, angry, or just unhappy with most situations. We probably have all known a Johnny Drama at one time, but we may not have realized that they were getting a natural high from the conflict. It is an unhealthy natural high since long-term exposure to this type of stress can cause a host of physical and psychological problems, like cancer, heart disease, and depression.

The Johnny Drama personality may be annoying to others, but it can be dangerous to the individual. Practicing relaxation techniques is a great way to reverse the body's stress response. These techniques can be as simple as breathing slowly and deeply when you're feeling overwhelmed, leaving the room when you're feeling angry, or removing yourself from a chronically stressful situation. The technique that works best for me is reframing a situation. When things are stressful, I am the king of negative thinking. Everything sucks and I find a reason why it is always going to suck. This type of thinking only makes a bad situation worse. The idea is not to compound your external stress (e.g., a car accident) with internal stress (e.g., "My car insurance will now be so expensive I won't be able to afford it!"). When I speak to my wife during these moments, she loves pointing out the negative trend in my thought pattern and encourages me to think of another explanation to counter my extremely negative one. Once I've come up with one or two alternative perspectives that are more objective or even positive, I tend to refocus and can calm down a bit.

CHAPTER SIX

Helping

"YOU EVER FIND YOURSELF BEING LAZY
FOR NO REASON AT ALL? LIKE YOU PICK UP YOUR MAIL,
YOU GO IN YOUR HOUSE, YOU REALIZE YOU HAVE A LETTER
FOR A NEIGHBOR -- YOU EVER JUST LOOK AT THE LETTER
AND GO, 'HM, LOOKS LIKE THEY'RE NEVER GETTING THIS.
TAKES TOO MUCH ENERGY TO GO OUTSIDE.'"
-JIM GAFFIGAN

What motivates the motivator? There are some days when I get up and feel like I would rather do nothing, days that I do not feel funny and do not want to perform. These feelings usually change the instant I see a good crowd waiting for me. But the travel is hard on the spirit. I can only take so many days in a row of waking up in a Hampton Inn and finding mystery hair in the shower before I start to lose it. I remember missing home so much once that I started to tear up during the Michael Buble' song, "I Want To Go Home." In my defense, that song could probably break Clint Eastwood.

The things that motivate me tend to be individuals who overcome circumstances far greater than mine in the name of helping other people. During my freshman year at Bucknell I met Steven Starkey, a young man so inspirational that just seeing him would change my mood for the rest of the day. Steven did not look like the other students at Bucknell. He was a heavy-set young man who wore a long beard and often dressed in sweats and a t-shirt. The great thing about him is he didn't seem fazed one bit that his clothes were not in fashion.

Steven lived on the same hall as some of my friends and it was easy to get to know him because all you needed to say was, "Hello." A conversation with Steven usually ended the same way every time – me walking away, him continuing to talk and me waving goodbye so as not to hurt his feelings. I soon learned that he was diagnosed with a brain tumor during his junior year in high school. It was inoperable and would one day take his life. He knew this and despite all of it was at college anyway. The doctors gave him chemotherapy and tried to shrink it, but they could not remove it. The tumor eventually grew and pushed against the speech and motor areas of his brain, impairing his functioning. When Steven walked, he walked very slowly dragging one leg behind him. When he talked, he slurred his speech and you had to take time to understand him. Everything about Steven was in slow motion on a campus that moved very fast. I was told that the medications he took made him tired and it was hard for him to stay awake at night to study. They also left him feeling exhausted every morning and his roommate told me just how impossible it was getting him up for class. By all accounts, Steven had a life that was far too hard for someone so young.

What inspired me about Steven was that, despite his illness, he was still at college. At the age of 18, there were about a dozen things I would have rather been doing than going to college. Not Steven. He was studying to become a teacher and he was an active member of a service fraternity and a religious group on campus. His life was literally about helping others or preparing to help others. He was doing all of these things while dealing with the insensitive reactions of those who did not know his story. I can recall seeing someone complain about being stuck behind Steven on their way up a flight of stairs because she was late to class. I remember seeing a student knock into him with a book bag and not even apologize. He dealt with this day, after day, after day. I was lucky enough to know Steven and every time I would see him in the hall or on the quad, his presence was motivating to me. My problems would fade away because I realized that Steven's reality was far tougher than mine and his problems much scarier.

The night before graduation, the Class of 1996 and their families filled the Weis Performing Arts Center for the Achievement Awards Ceremony. I was never big on awards, but since I was getting one I thought I would show up. It actually felt great to be recognized for my hard work as a social activist on campus. The final award that night was presented to the student who "...earned his degree while overcoming tremendous obstacles." When they announced Steven Starkey, there was the initial round of cordial applause, but no sign of Steven. Several seconds passed and I could see him starting to make his way slowly to the stage. As he limped and lumbered his way down the isle, the applause began to build. It erupted into a standing ovation. I imagined that the guilt of so many students who had dismissed Steven for 4 years was now coming to the surface. He accepted his award with that same expression on his face. I just wish he would have taken the mic and starting talking like he used to do with me.

Steven Starkey died in February of 1998. We had lost touch after college, but I understand from friends that after graduation he was working on finishing his teaching certification. The image of Steven is still fresh in my mind. He represented more than just hard work and persistence. Steven represented the importance of helping others. Steven may not have always had a happy life, but because he spent his time on this earth serving others I do believe he had a good life. His goodness comes back to me every time I lose perspective on my problems. Every time I wake up feeling not funny or lazy, I think of Steven. I remember what he stood for and even if I am lumbering, I get out of bed and try to help other people.

Big Tip Night
One example of a natural high that I never would have experienced without my friends from T.I.G.S. was "Big Tip Night." I learned the hard way that you've got to say that one slowly in front of an audience. The idea was simple. We gathered together about 10 friends and decided to go out for ice cream. In New Jersey we have

these places called Friendly's, which is a sit down ice cream place that serves great sundaes. We decided to arrive about 20 minutes before they closed, knowing that seeing a huge group of teenagers at that time would ruin any wait staff's night at Friendly's. Before we went in everyone chipped in an extra $5-$10 each for the tip. By the time we were done we had about $75 on what would be a $50 bill. I cannot remember having more fun eating ice cream, because of course, we were loud and laughing like crazy knowing what was about to happen. Once we finally finished, we put the money in a card and my friend filled it out with the greeting, "We think the best way to make the world a better place is to do good things for people." Then we all signed the card and made a quick exit. Once outside we did our best not to appear conspicuous, as we peeked inside and watched the reaction of our waitress. The smile on her face as she opened that card could have filled the room.

Exercise: Try your own version of Big Tip Night. If you do, let me know how it goes. I never would have been part of it without friends, so make sure you gather together a bunch of friends who like helping others. Write me at matt@mattbellace.com and let me know how it went.

Brain Facts: The Neurobiology of Helping Others

Human beings have the capacity for being selfish, but they also can show tremendous generosity towards strangers. The 2006 "Giving USA" survey revealed that, in 2006 alone, over $260 billion was given to U.S. charities, with three-quarters of that money coming from individuals. People give of their time, too. In 2005, over 65 million Americans volunteered to help charities.[1] Almost all volunteers surveyed reported that one of their motivations was "Feeling compassion toward other people." Despite all of the giving behavior, very little is known about the neurobiology of generosity and helping others.

It may be the case that generosity is part of human behavior because it helps sustain cooperative relationships. If you give to an organization during a time of need, perhaps the organization will help you during your time of need. Behavioral scientists have proposed that empathy plays the biggest role in helping behavior. Empathy is the ability to understand someone else's feelings. It is often described as "...putting yourself in someone else's shoes." Brain imaging studies in humans have shown that activities involving empathy and charitable giving activate regions in the brain that process emotional and social information, as well as the reward center.[2]

In a recent study, scientists in the Neuroeconomics Studies Department at Claremont Graduate University in California took a unique approach to investigating generosity.[3] They gave study participants a nose spray infused with the neuropeptide oxytocin, which is a neurochemical known to play a role in forming social attachments and feelings of love. Half of the study participants received oxytocin in the spray and half received a placebo (i.e., salt water). Compared to the placebo group, the group that received the oxytocin spray was 80% more generous in a task that involved giving away money to a stranger than those given a placebo. The generous participants left the experiment with less money, but many reported positive feelings associated with their generosity. These positive feelings are consistent with the effects of oxytocin on the reward center of the brain, which is known to induce dopamine release. If you receive a little reward from the brain – in the form of a natural high – by giving, you are more likely to give again.

Consistent with recent research, a study by Tankersley and colleagues showed that when people do good things (i.e., philanthropists), a part of the brain called the posterior superior temporal cortex (pSTC) is activated.[4] This part of the brain governs our altruistic behaviors and perceptions of social relationships. It is believed that some people have a more developed pSTC than others. However, it is not known if those with a highly developed pSTC do selfless things, or if those doing selfless things develop a more active pSTC. We do know that selfless actions create more of the "feel good" chemicals (e.g., dopamine) in the brain, and the brain is capable of growing and reshaping (i.e., neurogenesis) based on our behaviors. Therefore, if you want to improve upon your ability to help others – and receive a natural high from doing so – you need to start training your brain by helping more people and being empathetic to the pain of others.

Learning to Help: Really?
Yes, you can learn to be a person who helps others. Even if you were not raised in a family that valued helping other people, I believe you can still learn to do so. Neuroscientists believe the brain can be trained to help others and feel empathy for them. In my opinion, anyone who helps others – particularly helping the less fortunate – needs to receive something from the experience. I'm not talking about money. I am not even talking about building your resume. If you are truly going to be someone who helps others on a routine basis, you need to feel something positive from the experience. Helping is a natural high. Once you experience that high, it is important to engage in helping behaviors on at least a somewhat regular basis. This will allow you to truly experience the positive rewards that helping others can bring to you and to those whose lives you are impacting.

Interview: Jamie Sierfeld
I interviewed the director of the Lindsey Meyer Teen Institute (LMTI), the drug and alcohol prevention and leadership program in New Jersey that I mentioned in the first chapter. Jamie Sierfeld has been with the program since its inception and was a student in the program as well. She reflected on the large numbers of alumni – including myself – who have come through the teen institute program as high school students and went on to careers in the helping professions (e.g., teachers, counselors, social workers, psychologists). The first question I asked was whether she gets a natural high from helping others and if so, what does it feel like?

"I get a natural high from helping people – it feels good. For me, the highlight of the year is putting together the week-long leadership conference in August. [LMTI has over 300 high school students participate in an intensive week of training and motivation.] The natural high comes when I get a chance to stand back from the tent and reflect on how we put the entire week together. I know I've had a natural high

because I lose track of time and I notice that the little things bother me much less."

I also asked her to provide examples of evidence that the program can transform students into young people who are motivated to help others.

"At LMTI, we see transformations all the time. If I had not gotten involved in TIGS [i.e., Teen Institute of the Garden State, the original name of this prevention and leadership program], there is no way I would have ever chosen this career path. I think the reason so many students go on to work in the helping professions is that LMTI gives concrete examples of the what people do in helping professions. For example, high school students usually have an abstract idea what a counselor or social worker does, but when they come to camp and work with these individuals in small groups they see how rewarding it can be."

Helping is Meaningful Work

> *"Meaningful work is one of the most important things
> we can impart to children. Meaningful work is work that is
> autonomous. Work that is complex – that occupies your mind.
> And work where there is a relationship between effort and reward –
> for everything you put in, you get something out…"*
> -Malcolm Gladwell

I departed from using a comedian's quote here because Gladwell's quote is so true, so meaningful in itself, that it deserves sharing with my readers. In my opinion, there are few things more meaningful than helping others, especially those less fortunate than you are. For me, helping others means getting in front of groups of students and parents across the country and making them laugh with a message about wellness. For you, perhaps it means working in a biology lab looking for a cancer cure or being a field worker with Family Services trying to protect children from abuse. There is inherent meaning in trying to reach out to another human being in need and provide education, assistance, medical service, or just friendship.

Jamie Sierfeld described tremendous meaning behind her work. The Lindsey Meyer Teen Institute is named after a special young woman who participated in the program as a high school student and returned as a youth counselor. That is special enough, but she did all of this while suffering from Cystic Fibrosis – a rare genetic disease of the secretory glands that is life-shorting. Jamie was close friends with Lindsey and knew first hand what a tremendous impact she had on others.

Lindsey passed away far too young at the age of 17. Her wonderful parents took a risk and attempted a double lung transplant, each giving one of their own lungs to her in the hopes it would extend Lindsey's life. She faced the surgery like she faced everything in her life – with a sense of humor and determination. I recall interviewing Lindsey for the youth counselor position months before the surgery. I told her, "There are strict rules for attending the counselor trainings. If you miss one, you're out." She looked at me with these big eyes and said, "I may get a lung transplant soon, which means I may miss some of the trainings. Is that ok?" Holding back a smile I said, "No, they are very strict. Next question...." She pled her case, "But I need an operation!" I said, "I'm sorry it's final." I could only keep a straight face for so long and then we both burst out laughing because she knew I was kidding.

Today, LMTI is part of the Lindsey Meyer Foundation. In Jamie's words:

"For me, there is great meaning in working for the Lindsey Meyer Foundation. I get to help high school students address problems in their schools and communities, but I also get to give back to Lindsey and her family."

Summary

Helping others can actually produce a natural high similar to highs like running, eating, or laughing. Helping behavior can be learned through role models, family, or organizations dedicated to helping others. If you choose a career in the helping professions, you might not be rewarded with a large income, but you will provide yourself with something very special – meaningful work. It has been said that those who love what they do and engage in meaningful work never really work a day in their life.

CHAPTER SEVEN

Loving

"SHE PROPOSED TO ME. HOW WEIRD IS THAT?
IT WASN'T THOUGHTFUL. IT WASN'T ROMANTIC. SHE JUST
CAME IN AND SAID IT: 'LISTEN, UH – I'M PREGNANT.'"
-PETE DOMINICK

As an 8-year-old I thought girls were pretty gross and I suspect they didn't think much of me either. It wasn't until the hormones kicked in during the middle school years that I found myself wanting to talk on the phone with girls every night. Up until then the phone was used strictly for ordering pizzas and talking to Nana. Suddenly, in middle school I was compelled to engage in these oddly long conversations with girls about nothing. I believe that nature made loving another person one of the most powerful natural highs in existence for one reason – the survival of the species. In my case, I wish someone would have told me in middle school that it would be 15 years before I had a romantic relationship that would lead to marriage. It would have saved me a lot of phone calls.

The natural high of loving takes 3 major forms: romantic love, platonic love, and maternal love. Romantic love encompasses everything from your first crush in school to the 50th wedding anniversary. The natural high of falling in love is so powerful that it can make you do illogical things, like ride your bike 12 miles in the rain just to hang out with Kristi Carrara on a hot summer night. I'm not saying I did that (in August of 1990), but it could happen. The highest highs of romantic love may come during the first few weeks of a new relationship, but the most meaningful highs tend to surface over years of commitment and building a life together. In some cases, romantic love leads to a child. Maternal love – or paternal love for dads – is one of the strongest motivators of parents to protect their infants. As I write this book, I cannot say that I've experienced paternal love. However, I can appreciate how special it must be because all too often parents will give you 80 reasons why having a child is miserable and then end with, "Oh, but I love it so much." The final loving natural high comes from having an amazing friendship or relationship with a person or pet that is neither romantic nor maternal or paternal. It is one of those relationships that improves the quality of your life and makes you feel great. To me, a great friend is someone you could have fun with while merely waiting on line.

Romantic Love Story

"I knew it was time to get engaged because I couldn't take vacations anymore. I would say to my girlfriend, 'Let's go to Italy.' She would just look at me and say, 'I want to go to Zales.' I thought, 'Ok, is there a direct flight there?'"
-Matt Bellace

In high school and college, I spent so much time in relationships, trying to get into relationships, or trying to get out of relationships that you would have thought I was getting credits for it. I am not sure what the point of all of it was except to prove to myself that I had trouble being alone during those years. It may be the case that I was a little too into the natural high that accompanies new romantic relationships. Addicted is too strong a word, because it never interfered with my academics or other activities, but it was certainly a distraction. I just think the novelty of the new relationship is tremendously exciting, but that excitement can work for or against you.

In college, I met this beautiful Italian American girl named Kristy. She was a fellow biology student and we met while making photocopies. I guess it was love at first collate. She had such a sweet voice and big eyes like a Japanese Anime cartoon that I could not resist striking up a conversation. Fortunately, women seem to know within seconds of meeting a guy if they are interested, so as long as I wasn't Bin Laden I was cool. We went out a few times and it was great. We had such a cool chemistry together that each date was more fun than the next. It wasn't long before I found myself having long conversations with her about nothing and doing illogical things.

Kristy and I dated for the next year and a half. We had great some great times together and even began introducing each other to our families. However, the relationship was complicated by life events – like us attending graduate schools 3 hours apart and me traveling often. I had a friend who once said, "The right person at the wrong time is still the wrong person." I think Kristy and I met each other at the wrong time, but the illogical romantic love thing still convinced me, "She's the one."

The day Kristy dumped me was like any other. We had been having discussions about transferring graduate schools to live closer to each other, but I could tell that it was not going anywhere. The call came during the afternoon and I was...well, I was on the toilet. For some reason, I felt compelled to hobble to the phone, pants around my ankles and pick up the call. She immediately gave me the, "We've got to talk..." line. I was really in no state for a long conversation, but I was alone so I thought, "Let's do this." She explained that the relationship was not working for her and that she needed a "break." I don't remember much after that except how short the call was and how quickly it was over forever. I made my way back to the bathroom and with the timing of a comedic actor, I tripped and fell on my sad pathetic face.

It took a few days for the pain to really settle in. When it did I decided to call Kristy for a better explanation (a.k.a., the try to get back together with her call). When we dated, we used to call each other every night at 10 PM. It was our time. For the next week, I called at 10 PM and no one answered. I left a message each time and grew increasingly impatient. Finally, after 2 weeks someone picked up the phone. It was a male's voice and Kristy lived alone. I asked who it was and he said his name was Matt. The irony of his name was quickly lost on me as I remembered that Kristy had been talking about a Matt that started working in her lab. It was him – I was sure of it. I don't know why he was there, but I don't think it was to make coffee. I left a message and as soon as I hung up completely lost all sense of logic. The natural high of romantic love had become a natural low. I was so crazy that I made plans to blow off the next day and drive 3 hours that night to see her. Fortunately, a friend talked me down, but the pain of doing nothing was still devastating. The emotional pain was as strong as seeing a loved one die. I felt guilty for feeling that way, but I could not control it.

The best advice I was given during that time came from a movie called Swingers. The advice was simple: "Do not call, e-mail, or go see this girl ever again – no matter how much it hurts. In time, she will contact you." I went 14 months, 2 weeks, and 1 day without contacting Kristy – not that I was keeping track. Actually, it was torture. Everything that reminded me of her suddenly became a reason to get depressed. Can you imagine getting bummed out every time you saw a red Ford Focus? I was convinced that I would never be happy again.

One random August day, Kristy contacted me through a mutual friend and asked if we could meet. It almost seemed too similar to the movie. I agreed to get together and I am glad I did. The meeting was a roller coaster of emotions, but it had a profound effect on my life. When I left I felt as though a weight had been lifted off my chest. I no longer thought Kristy was the one. I will always have feelings for her, but on that day it just felt different. She wanted to get back together and I just could not see it. I had been dating someone for a few months and somehow seeing Kristy solidified for me that this new relationship represented the future. In the weeks following our meeting, I thought about Kristy less and less. It's funny how life works because the girl I was dating at the time eventually became my wife.

Paternal Love Story

*"My pregnant wife cries a lot, needs to eat every few hours,
and is constantly in the bathroom.
People ask me, 'When's the baby due?' I say, 'It's already here.'"*
-Matt Bellace

My wife and I decided to have a child in 2008. We had been married for over five years and it felt like it was time. We tried for a few months and things were not happening, so my wife said, "You should go to the doctor." I said, "Why me? What about you?" When I was in the doctor's office he ordered a semen analysis. I said to him, "My wife and I are both psychologists. This kid is going to be analyzed its entire life already. Do you have to start in my scrotum?" The results came back and the actual report read, "Matt's sperm are slow and have big heads." Apparently my sperm are from Texas. The doctor was looking at me like it was my fault. I had no explanation. I don't know why a lifetime of avoiding drugs and alcohol gave me Seth Rogan's sperm.

The doctor informed me that the condition could be corrected with a minor procedure. I told him that nothing that involves cutting into me down there is "minor." He called it "microsurgery," which is kind of a diss. I asked him, "What anesthesia do you use? He said, "Oh, it's mild." I said, "No, you're going to induce a coma. Listen to me Dr. House, I want no part of this recovery. Wake me up in a year."

In the end, the procedure went well and a week later I was recovering nicely. I called my cousin to tell him how things went and he picked up the phone with his 1-year-old boy screaming in the background. I told him what happened. He said, "What? You got cut for this?" and he held the phone up to his crying infant. "You should have told the doctor to cut deeper. It would have saved you a lot of trouble." Two months later my wife was pregnant.

As I write this my wife is still pregnant, so I do not know about paternal love just yet. However, as I watch my wife deal with all the inconveniences of pregnancy, I am reminded of a study on fraternity hazing. Psychologists learned that the more fraternity brothers suffered to gain acceptance into the fraternity, the more they reported enjoying the experience of being a fraternity brother. It makes sense. If they didn't like being a fraternity brother it would mean that what they went through was a waste of time. I think the foundation for maternal love must include all the things a mother has to go through to have the child. Once that child is born a bond begins to form, but in many ways the bond was forming for nine months. My wife and I know nothing about being parents yet, but we do know that the idea of being parents seems like such a powerful natural high that we agreed to go through with it in the first place.

Platonic Love Story
Platonic love encompasses all other forms of love that are not romantic or parental. This form of the natural high can include love for a grandparent, a pet, or even a mentor that helped you through a tough time. It can be love for the game of baseball, traveling, or a house that you helped to create. In my life, I have experienced love for all of these things. It is hard to say when the feelings of love began, but I always knew how much love I had in my heart the moment one of these people or experiences was gone.

The day I learned that my Pop's cancer was terminal I immediately ran into my mother's arms and cried. The tears were strong and would not stop. Pops was an iconic figure in my family and he could not be replaced. He had always made me the center of attention when I was around him. In fact, he had put off the CAT scan – which would ultimately diagnose his cancer – by a few days just so we could spend time golfing during my spring break. He was like the glue that held my family together.

Pops had a certain way about him that just seemed to make people want to be near him. I can remember staying with my Nana and Pops on vacation and seeing how much he was in constant social demand. He was the former mayor of Point Pleasant, NJ and one of the reasons the town is such a hot spot on the Jersey Shore in the summertime. He also owned an Oldsmobile dealership with this brother. As a result, over the years I heard so many stories of business and family men helped through hard times by Pops. In some cases, he would loan cars to people in need so they could get a job. People loved my grandfather so much that – unsolicited – they would tell me about it. There would be moments when I would be hanging around the car dealership and some stranger would stop me and say, "Your grandfather Roy is such a special man. I hope you realize." I really did.

I can vividly recall sleeping over my grandparents' house in the final days of Pop's life. I was praying to God and scolding him for allowing this to happen to my grandfather. At one point, I asked that my life be taken so such a great man could be spared. Of course, it was futile. Pops passed away soon after and I was left to make sense of it. Someone I met at the funeral gave me the advice to incorporate my favorite aspects of Pops into my own personality. It was then that I decided that I would do what I could to make a difference in other people's lives, just like Pops did. I have spent the last 21 years pursuing that goal – one that I will never fully complete. As much as I wish I could become Pops, I can only keep him in my memories while I try to be a better version of myself.

While I was in middle school, I decided to wake up each morning and go running to get into better shape. If I didn't feel like doing it one morning, I thought of how courageous Pops was while battling his cancer. In high school, I decided to play 3 sports – football, wrestling, and baseball. When someone would make fun of me for being too small, too weak, or too white, I would try to emulate Pop's positive attitude. In college, I founded a student prevention group and was told I was committing "social suicide." When the prevention work would get me down, I remembered stories about how courageous Pops was while running for mayor of Point Pleasant. He was the first Italian American mayor of the town – no small feat in the late 1950's. Given all of this history, it might not come as a surprise that when my wife and I learned we were going to have a boy, she said to me, "Let's name it after your grandfather because he meant so much to you." I cannot describe how wonderful it felt to hear her say those words. So we're calling him Grandpa. I think it's unique. "Let me introduce Grandpa Bellace. He's the real Benjamin Button."

Exercise: Think about a loved one that you have lost. If you are lucky enough not to have lost anyone, then think of someone you admire. Pick 1 or 2 positive traits of that individual and ask yourself, "How can I incorporate those traits into my everyday life?" It may surprise you to experience just how great it feels to carry on the memory of loved one in such a meaningful way.

Brain Facts: Neurobiology of Love

Romantic love and maternal love are considered natural highs because they are both highly rewarding experiences. In terms of brain functioning, these two types of attachment activate overlapping regions within the brain's reward system and release feel good chemicals. In the case of romantic love, vasopressin, oxytocin, and dopamine have been shown to be released in response to romantic feelings (Zeki, 2007). Maternal love also releases these chemicals, but the brain activated brain areas are slightly different (thank goodness). Maternal love produces stronger activation in the part of the brain that is specific for faces. This is consistent with the importance of a mother's ability to read her child's facial expressions and determine how the child is feeling. Interestingly, mothers who give birth without pain medications have been shown to release endorphins, which are morphine-like substances made by the body to relieve pain. Long distance runners and athletes may also experience this pain and enjoy the runner's high as previously discussed.

In my opinion, comparisons between the feelings of natural childbirth and the runner's high should only be made by women who have experienced both. A friend, fellow psychologist, and marathon runner, Talia Zaider recently gave birth to her first child without the use of pain killers. I asked her to describe any comparisons between her experiences with natural childbirth and running a marathon.

"In some ways the high is similar because it's the release you feel from intense and often painful exertion - both in completing the New York City marathon and in giving birth, my body was pushed past any familiar limit and that felt tremendously powerful. The main difference I think is that when I gave birth to Zoe, the high was shared, it enveloped both of us so that we were in total synch. It felt more like the knees-weak feeling of being head over heels in love. Tim says that when Zoe started to come out, the midwife said, 'now take your baby!' and I literally pulled her out of me with my own hands and brought her up to my chest. I have absolutely no recollection of doing that, I may have even done it with my eyes closed. He said he saw a look on my face of complete calm like I was totally transfixed with her and the rest of the world just melted away. That's kind of how I feel holding her now. So while running distances, there is a euphoria that is entirely bound within yourself as an individual, whereas the euphoria of birth draws you into an almost urgent connection with another."

It does seem as though comparisons between natural childbirth and the runner's high are reasonable, but not perfect. Talia's comments suggest that the natural high of childbirth elicits deeper feelings, particularly when the pain and exertion are over. It also seems that completing a marathon is a mostly individual experience, although you could certainly run with friends and bring a more social element to it. However, childbirth seems to involve the unique element of bonding with your newborn child. It is also notable that Tim's statement that Talia had a look of "complete calm" suggests that she could have been experiencing the positive effects of the neurotransmitter oxytocin.

If you have ever been in love you may not be surprised to learn that romantic love can bring madness into your life. For example, you may find yourself obsessed with that person – thinking about them much more than you would normally think about another human being. It turns out that there is a biological basis for that obsession. An increase in dopamine is often coupled with a decrease in the neurotransmitter serotonin, which is linked to mood. Recent research has shown that serotonin levels in the brains of a people who are in love are similar to that of the levels seen in patients with

Obsessive-Compulsive Disorder.[1] The next time you find yourself unable to concentrate because you cannot stop thinking about a romantic partner, remember it is just part of the wonderful experience of being alive and in love.

Have you ever known someone who has lost a love – whether it is due to break up or death – and cannot let go of thinking of them? They may talk about the person so much that you may ask yourself, "What are they getting from this?" The grieving process is different for each person and the amount of grieving that is healthy may depend on how long you knew the person and the type of relationship. For example, grieving for a spouse of 50 years will likely be different than grieving after breaking up with a girl that you dated for 6 weeks.

Prolonged and enduring grief can develop into what is called complicated grief. This is grief that used to be referred to as chronic, pathological, or traumatic. A recent study found that the brains of individuals who experience complicated grief show activation in the reward pathways.[2] In fact, some scientists have hypothesized that this type of attachment to the grieving process may have addiction-like properties.[3] While some degree of grieving can be appropriate and healthy, one must be cautious about falling into a pattern in which they become addicted to the grieving process and the benefits that they may be experiencing from maintaining this process.

Summary: Lucky to Love
Compared to other natural highs, the brain has slightly different mechanisms for achieving the high associated with love. The experience of love activates the brain's reward center, which releases the neurotransmitters vasopressin and oxytocin. The natural high of love is truly unlike any other.

This chapter is unlike any other in this book. Unfortunately, I cannot provide you with advice on how to achieve the natural high of love, and have not provided excerpts of interviews with "experts" on loving. No exercise can help bring it to you. Yet, if you are able to experience love in its romantic, platonic, and/or maternal forms you should consider yourself quite lucky. In my life, I have known people who have experienced all forms of love and some who seem to have experienced none. I have known miserable people who unfortunately cannot appreciate all the loved ones in their life, and happy people who don't understand why they cannot seem to find love. I have known parents who could seem to care less about their children, and married couples who will do anything to have children of their own.

Luck seems to be a big factor in whether or not love finds you, but you are the factor in whether or not you enjoy love. I can tell you that if you are lucky enough to experience the love of a pet, a friend, girlfriend, boyfriend, or child, you should not take it for granted. If there are things you've always wanted to do with your loved one, do not put them off. Make plans today to take that trip or have that picnic or just go to a ballgame. Love is to be cherished because time is always a limiting factor in our lives. In time, loved ones will move away, pass away, or grow apart. What makes love so special is that it is not guaranteed to any of us.

CHAPTER EIGHT

Creating – Your Own Natural High

"I THINK THE ONLY REASON MY JEWISH WIFE MARRIED
ME IS BECAUSE I HAVE A PHD. ON THE GENTILE TO JEWISH
CONVERSION TABLE, 'DOCTOR' IS A MATCH."
-MATT BELLACE

I decided in fourth grade that I wanted to be a doctor, but I had no idea what type. My only problem was figuring out how to fit in all the schooling while also playing shortstop for the New York Yankees. Fortunately, Derek Jeter came along and made it easier for me to focus on the doctor thing. I received a PhD in Clinical Psychology from Drexel University in June 2005, 21 years after the fourth grade daydream. Receiving a doctoral degree after so many years was one of the most intense natural highs I have ever experienced. The reason it was so intense was because of all the obstacles that seemed to stand in the way during my journey.

There are surely many more natural highs than the short list of scientifically proven natural highs presented in the various chapters of this book. Achieving a goal can be a powerful natural high, but I do not have the brain scans to prove it. The day I graduated from Drexel, I felt the most euphoric I had ever felt before in my life. I was giddy to the point of being annoying to others around me. I guess there was just something extra special about earning something that no one could take away from me. In retrospect, the glee of finishing my PhD was probably so powerful because of the struggle I went through to get it.

As a freshman at Bucknell University, I failed my first biology test. Let me rephrase that – I got a 38…out of 100! I really deserved an F-minus. To make matters worse, I had a friend who dropped out of the class because he got a 68 and didn't think he could pick his grade up enough to do well. If it sounds like a hard class, it wasn't. It was considered "baby bio," which meant that it was a class for non-biology majors. Real biology majors thought it was a joke, which was unfortunate because at the time I failed the test I was thinking of majoring in biology. I guess when it rains, it pours.

There were two roads I could have taken after getting the 38. I could have dropped the class and given up any dreams of majoring in biology. The other move would be to study constantly and just try to really learn the subject. I chose to stick it out and spent countless hours in the library. I studied harder than I ever had before and I ended up getting a C+ for the semester – not bad, considering. I was no Rhodes Scholar and my GPA would never impress anyone, but those days taught me that no matter how down I was hard work made a difference. Biology had been something I loved learning about since the whole spider plant project in third grade. So why should I give it up just because I wasn't perfect?

Eventually I took enough biology classes to qualify for the major. During those classes, I watched all the cut-throat pre-med students fight to get their A minuses bumped up. One student was so excited he yelled, "I got it up to a 97!" while his entire face would twitch because of nervous tics. I wanted to tell him, "Dude, getting an A is not worth making my face look like that."

The truth is I had some real anxiety of my own. Each exam in the higher levels of biology revealed my psychological weaknesses. I studied harder and harder, but when it came time for the tests I was missing questions on information that I had studied. I think it was because I was completely distracted by everything in the room. This one guy was so nervous he used to chew his nails like a dog chewing a bone. It would make this disgusting, wet, popping sound. I would have said something, but he was such a nice guy I felt bad. This other girl used to finish the tests in half the time it took everyone else to finish, and then she would make all this noise while leaving the room. What an attention-seeking-pain-in-my-butt move! There is nothing more demoralizing than struggling on number two while Usain Bolt over there is zippering up her bag.

My test taking anxiety got so bad that I eventually went to a psychologist on campus to talk about my struggles. His name was Dr. Eric Afsprung and he had the quietest office I had ever seen. He was such a calming person that I couldn't think of a better psychologist to calm my weary nerves. At first, we discussed whether or not it could be a learning disability. Of course, I went right for the self-defeating "I'm just not smart enough to be here" angle. What a load of crap. It turns out neither one was likely. As we explored things further, it turned out that it was my test taking anxiety that was affecting my scores. Dr. Afsprung wrote a letter to my professors asking them if I could take my exams in a quiet room. As soon as I did, my grades went up and suddenly I felt better about my academic performance. It is amazing that a simple change of room could change my grades. The semester that I saw Dr. Afsprung was also the semester I took a class that would change my career. It was called Physiological Psychology and it focused on the nervous system and behavior. Ironically, it was a psychology class and it was taught by this wonderful professor, Dr. Owen Floody. His approach to teaching this class was so much different than the memory overload we got in biology classes. Dr. Floody took his time to really think about the material, and he expected his students to do the same. Some students hated it. They thought it was dry and boring, but I was never more into a class in my life. Over the next few years, I took every course Owen Floody taught at Bucknell. My favorite was Human Neuropsychology, which helped me to realize what type of doctor I wanted to be – a neuropsychologist.

Into the Wild

"In California, they have towns named after their natural beauty,
like 'Mountain View' or 'Pebble Beach.'
You'll never see that in New Jersey
because then we'd have towns called,
'Weird Smell' and 'Dead Body.'"
-Matt Bellace

The John Krakauer book Into the Wild was turned into the 2007 movie by the same name because it captured a human instinct – to get back to nature. I highly recommend the book or the film because it shows how fulfilling (and yet nutty) the idea of leaving modern society can be for someone. It may not be the typical natural high, but there are many positive emotions associated with putting yourself into an environment where your senses matter more than your bank account.

Interview with Paul Brown

One of my oldest friends from high school, Paul Brown, created his own natural high and made a career out of it. Paul's natural high is experiencing wildlife up close. In New Jersey, "wildlife" usually includes things like a parrot on someone's shoulder or the animals that live in people's garbage. Despite this, from an early age Paul exhibited an interest in all things outdoors. I found it interesting to learn that no one in his family fostered this love for the wild – it was his own thing that he just picked up. Paul attended Ramapo College in New Jersey where he studied environmental science. After graduation, he was volunteering with a hawk watch in New Jersey and working at an outdoor store, but dreamed of heading west. In my opinion, Paul seemed miserable living and working a non-wildlife-related job in New Jersey. The only time he perked up was when we were fishing, or when he talked about traveling to places like Utah, Wyoming, and Colorado. Here is Paul in his own words commenting on the first time he went out west:

"Seeing snow in the summer and smelling that mountain air blew me away. I fell in love easily with the wildlife and the sense of wilderness. You realize that when you're not on top of the food chain, you have to use all of your senses – like smell and hearing. I loved it."

Paul first lived in Utah and got a job with the Forest Service, but soon ran out of money and had to return home to plan how he would make a living. On a vacation to Jackson, Wyoming to visit his friend he discovered the place that would eventually bring him back – Yellowstone National Park. Yellowstone was the nation's first national park and is roughly the size of Delaware and Rhode Island combined. At least that is what Paul tells me.

"Moving back to New Jersey was a big letdown. I was not happy and I missed the feeling of being around so much wildlife. It was depressing to work at a job just to make money. It was actually dreadful."

What always fascinated me about Paul's story was that despite his depressed feelings, he took a risk and did something about his situation. There are so many people who become paralyzed when they realize that they are miserable in their own life. They do nothing and think things will change.

"If you really want something you can make it work. It helped that I was young and had the desire to experience different things."

It took me a little while to hone in on the specific aspects of the wildlife natural high. I have to admit that thanks to Paul, I have had the opportunity to experience several of these during trips to Jackson, WY. One of the hallmarks of this natural high is losing your sense of time. Forgetting exactly what day it is or how long you have been doing something is a marker for just how much you are into an experience. Paul describes his wildlife natural high:

"I get an instant adrenaline rush when I spot wolves. If I'm taking guests out on a tour and we see some wolves, I get very excited because it is fun

watching others get psyched. These are rare animals that people traveled thousands of miles to see and I am showing it to them – that is a natural high. If the animals break into a chase, my heart races, I starting talking really fast, and I lose all track of time."

Meditating

As an eighth grader, I had two things going for me – I was athletic and tall. Well, I have never been tall, but at five·foot eight I was tall-ish for eighth grade. My problem was that I would only grow one more inch over the next five years of growing. It's not my fault. I am tall for an Italian. I'm like Shaq in Italy.

I played center on my community league basketball team in eighth grade. (Calling it a team was being generous, because we had like two kids who could shoot.) During one game I scored 70 points and we won 72 to 70. I guess I was a bit of ball hog. The point is that I was an amazing basketball player for one year of my life. It was the year before kids my age grew and the year I learned to meditate.

We had a motivational speaker come to address the league and I remember one thing about his talk. He said players who visualized themselves making baskets in the game before they went out to play were proven to score more points than those who did not visualize. It turned out to be great advice. Prior to games, I started crawling into the closet in my room, turning out the lights, and visualizing myself scoring points and winning the game. Our team went from average to competing for the league championship in about a month. I can still recall how peaceful it felt to walk into the arena prior to games after my little mediation sessions. It was like nothing bothered me. There was almost no anxiety – and no question in my mind that I could win the game.

I certainly would not say that my little basketball meditation experiment is proof that meditation works. First of all, no one showed me what to do or talked me through the visualization. However, I believed so much in visualizing in a dark room that I even used it again later in life. The first several times I started doing stand-up comedy I used visualization to walk myself through my set. I would visualize the stage, the audience, and me – crushing of course. The first time I tried the exercise, I was doing a gig at the Pizzeria Uno's off of South Street in Philadelphia. There were no dark rooms there, so I made sure to meditate at home. It was a big night. My in-laws were in the crowd and I wanted them to know I was the best comedian to ever work a Pizzeria Uno's. The gig was actually a lot of fun for me, partly because the audience was good and I slowed down my pace. In my previous sets, I would speak so fast that I was stepping on the laughs. But the Uno's gig was different. I was so calm and focused that I was really able to be in the moment and make my act feel very natural.

Calm is a state of natural high. Many people use drugs to reach a sense of calm, but fortunately there are calming highs all around us. If meditation is not your thing, you should consider traveling to places where the atmosphere is high in negative ions. These are odorless, tasteless, and invisible molecules that we inhale in abundance in certain environments. Think mountains, waterfalls, and beaches. Once they reach our bloodstream, negative ions are believed to produce biochemical reactions that increase levels of the mood chemical serotonin. In turn, serotonin helps to alleviate feelings of depression, relieve stress, and boost our daytime energy.

Exercise: If you live near a beach, mountains, or waterfalls, this experiment could be interesting for you. The next time you are about to embark on a day trip – to the beach, let's say – pay attention to the difference in your mood prior to leaving and once you return home at the end of the day. Are there any changes to how you feel physically and emotionally? Do you have a sense of calm? If you enjoy that process, you may want to learn more about meditation (which is easier than going to the beach) at www.tmeducation.org.

Brain Facts: The Meditating Brain
There are many documented benefits of meditation, including improved immune functioning, deeper sleep, reduced levels of anxiety, and improved mood.[1,2,3] In recent years, meditative practices have been implemented in hospitals and academic medical centers to help soothe patients with chronic stress and pain-related

disorders. Neuroscientists have also become interested in the relationships between meditation, brain activity, and immune system functioning.

Stressful life events have been shown to negatively impact the benefits of receiving a flu shot.[4] Researchers studied this phenomenon by measuring the amount of antibodies produced following the flu shot in individuals experiencing chronic stressors like caring for a spouse with dementia. Normally, when someone receives the flu vaccine their antibody levels increase. However, caregivers showed a poorer antibody response following vaccination relative to a control group of non-chronically stressed individuals. Based on this result, researchers at the Laboratory of Affective Neuroscience at University of Wisconsin hypothesized that meditation might have the opposite effect on immune functioning.[1] To test their idea, they measured antibody titers in individuals who underwent an 8-week trial of meditation. They also measured brain electrical activity before, immediately after, and 4 months following the meditation training. They found significant increases in flu vaccine antibody titers after receiving the shot in those who received the meditation training, as compared with a control group. In addition, measures of brain electrical activity showed increased activity in the anterior left hemisphere, an area shown in previous studies to be associated with positive affect.[5]

Learning to Create Your Own – Paintball
Creating your own natural high in part means being comfortable with trying new things and taking social risks. As I discussed in the first chapter, my inspiration for creating the student group C.A.L.V.I.N. & H.O.B.B.E.S. was that I was not happy as a Bucknell student. I was faced with a choice: I could either change my school and leave, or change the school and do something about it. If you are someone that never feels compelled to try something new or change your circumstances, then creating your own natural high might not be for you.

One of my favorite C&H events was paintball. Central PA has one of the best paintball facilities in the country, called Skirmish

USA in Jim Thorpe, PA. They have dozens of paintball fields with names like "Amazon Jungle" and "Z-Swamp." I do not remember which of our C&H members suggested the event, but when you have a group of 40-plus young people, you have the makings for a great event.

We had a great budget that semester and the paintball event generated a lot of buzz about our group on campus. Let's say it cost $30 per person, plus paint, transportation, and lunch for the day. Multiply that by 40 students and you have a nearly $2,000 event. The only problem was that we only had $1,000 and still needed to advertise. So, our brilliant idea was to guarantee that we would pay for 20 members to play and hold a raffle on campus for the other 20 spots – one dollar per ticket and the winners play for free. It was a huge success! The raffle generated an additional $1,000 because students were happy to risk a few dollars for a day that could easily cost $50.

The day of the event was one of those perfect fall days. We drove out to Jim Thorpe in vans and I watched as students sat quietly in their little cliques. Once we arrived, we split everyone up into 2 teams of 20. It turned out that we brought a big enough group to be assigned to our own field with our own officials. We spent the day battling around trees, crawling trough streams, and generally running around like maniacs in a capture-the-flag type event. At one point, I remember getting hit in that one spot that is not protected. No, not that one… It was actually my neck. When those paintballs hit my skin and burst, I looked down in panic and yelled, "Is it blood? Oh no, is it blood?" To which someone next to me said, "It's green."

The ride home from the event said it all. In the vans, there were no more barriers between people, just friends telling "war" stories. Everyone had bonded over a shared experience. We were all exhausted because we had gone through so many emotions on the field – fear, surprise, euphoria. I recall having so many students genuinely thankful that we had put on the event. It was almost as if they did not believe they could have that much fun in college.

Exercise: Dude, you've got to play paintball! If you are anywhere near Eastern Pennsylvania, check out Skirmish USA at www.skirmish. com. If not, there is bound to be a paintball field somewhere near you.

Learning to Create Your Own – New Mexico Student List
I recently spoke at several district student council conferences in New Mexico. One of the conferences was in Roswell, NM. On my way to Roswell friends told me, "You know what's in Roswell? They have aliens there." The 4-hour drive from Albuquerque (in the dark) was so mind numbingly straight that I could have fallen asleep and still arrived safely. I was about an hour outside of Roswell when it happened… I saw 6 or 7 lights dancing in the sky in a coordinated pattern. They would dart inward toward the middle and then out. I thought, "This is it…" It turned out be a Wal-Mart grand opening in the distance. Undies were half off that week.

During the conferences, I presented a workshop that involved students creating a list of natural high activities that they considered as much fun as going to a party. The events they came up with were creative, simple, and inexpensive. Here is the complied list from all of the groups:

- Movie Under the Stars
- Scavenger Hunt
- Sports Tournament
- Giant Slip-n-Slide Party
- Murder Mystery Party
- Open Mic / Coffee House
- Mud Volleyball Tournament
- Battle of the Bands
- Rock-n-Bowl
- Video Game Tournament
- Camping Trip
- Karaoke Party
- Lock-In, including many of the above activities

I purposely did not elaborate on these events because I think it is up to each individual group to define what their event will look like. If you have a small group, then suggesting that the National Guard come and dig mud trenches for your mud volleyball event is probably unrealistic! If you have over 500 students then a camping trip would really not be something that is logistically feasible. So, I suggest that each unique group apply their own local flavor to make any event special.

It seemed like quite a coincidence that, soon after compiling this list, I saw a television commercial for hard liquor that included people drinking at a giant slip-n-slide party. If you see the ad, you will notice that there is virtually nothing in the ad about alcohol, except that they paired it with a great slip-n-slide event. I find it flattering that alcohol companies are turning to natural highs to sell their products, but do they really need to spoil the true spirit of a natural high? This phenomenon is not a new one. When I was younger, they tried to convince us that alcohol would bring more loving natural highs involving young men and woman in bikinis. When I was in my 20's, the commercials seemed to be all about the laughter natural high, as the commercials took a decidedly funny turn. I do not expect the runner's high to be paired with alcohol any time soon. That could get ugly.

Exercise: If you have a group that is looking to put on a social event, try one of the events suggested by the New Mexico students. They can be tailored for groups of all ages. The older folks may need some supervision, but everyone else should be fine.

Outrunning Negativity

If you are going to attempt new things in life, like paintball, meditating, or eating new foods, you will probably face some level of resistance. Some of it may be well intended… like those who want you to avoid hypothermia when you're surfing Lake Erie in January. However, others will simply be projecting their own negative thoughts about the activity onto you by saying, "You can't do that!" or "What's wrong with you?" Unfortunately, this type of dismissive feedback from other can often put an end to a lot of positive risk-taking behaviors by putting people on the defensive.

I suggest 2 approaches to dealing with negative people when ignoring them is not an option. First, it will likely be helpful to let the person know how they make you feel. Doing so might make them more aware of what they are saying. When I was in college, I would often use the line, "Are you trying to be a jerk or are you just getting lucky?" Of course, you might find it more productive to say something like, "I don't really find your comments supportive. What would make you say something like that?" If you accompany your feedback with body language that suggests that you are not happy with their comments – like raised eyebrows and stepping back – it will help to emphasize your message. If the negative person does not seem to care that they have hurt your feelings, you may want to consider that the next time you think about sharing something with them.

A second approach to dealing with the chronically negative is to try to empathize with them. Yes, that is right – caring more about their feelings than they care about yours. Empathy, or putting yourself in someone else's shoes, can actually give you insight into what motivates their negativity. The person may have grown up in an abusive environment where negativity was the norm. They may be feeling miserable about their own current life situation, thereby making it difficult for them to be happy for you. They could also just be a jerk, but that explanation is far less interesting.

During a workshop at a youth summit in New Jersey, a high school teacher told a story about how negativity impacted her behavior. She shared with the group the details of her first sky diving experience, which she referred to as a "tremendous natural high." I don't doubt that she got naturally high. If you jump out of an airplane – and live – you will undoubtedly feel good about it. In fact, the key to getting a great natural high is choosing an activity that engages your emotions. Sky diving definitely fits that profile. I cannot imagine yawing during a sky dive. Well, the teacher landed safely and told us that she could not wait to tell everyone she knew about her experience. However, her story took a sad turn when she told us that her husband ruined the moment by "…being very negative about the entire experience." She told us that he could not understand her enthusiasm for the jump and "…picked and picked at it" until she didn't want to talk about it anymore. To steal a phrase, her husband was a natural high "buzz kill."

The woman did not tell her husband how he made her feel, which is unfortunate. She may have missed an opportunity to shed some light on how he was being perceived by others. If it were me, I probably would have attempted empathy. I would have tried to connect with the husband's legitimate fear that his wife could die from jumping out of a plane. It is possible that he spent the whole day worrying about her and instead of sharing those thoughts, he decided to be negative about the activity in the hopes that she would never do it again. Negativity like his is not an adaptive way for us to deal with our emotions, but unfortunately a lot of people choose that route. My advice in this case would be to come out and ask, "Are you being negative because you thought I was going to get hurt?" You might even encourage that person to come and witness the event first hand in order to see for themselves the precautions that are implemented by sky diving instructors.

Research shows that people who are constantly negative in the words they use and the reactions they have are probably not the most mentally healthy people (Mathews and MacLeod, 2005). Remember – you have a choice when it comes to who you lean on for emotional support. Finding people who love you and who will be there for you is important, but also look for people who themselves are happy individuals. People who have the ability to be genuinely happy for you are often those who can really listen to you when you have a problem.

Exercise: Make a list of the 5 most positive people and the 5 most negative people in your life. Then assign each person with a number from 0 to 5, 0 being the least positive/negative and 5 being the most positive/negative. When you are finished, examine each entry and write down why you gave each person the rating that you did. You may decide that, after creating your list, you have very few negative influences in your life. If this is unfortunately not the case, you may wish to distance yourself from some of those on your list who tend to bring you down. I did this exercise in ninth grade and found it gave me tremendous insight into my friends and family.

My Best Natural High Day

My birthday is in December, every year. Just once, it would be cool to have a birthday during a warm weather month or at least far away from a month during which everyone spends all of their money. When I was in my twenties, I used to think about the perfect day for my birthday and try to carry it out. I would hit my favorite restaurant at night and do a few things that I love doing in December, like sleeping late, reading, and picking out gifts for friends and family. Over the years, I expanded my "best day" to include each season.

Summer
Location: Beach house in Ocean City, NJ, La Jolla, CA, or any great beach spot
Morning:
1)   Wake up and surf for an hour or so – preferably with friends

2)   Have breakfast while reading the newspaper on the deck overlooking the ocean

3)   Go to the gym and workout…or take a nap

Afternoon:
4)   Sit on the beach, throw football around with friends

5)   Walk the beach or go for a swim in the waves

6)   End the day by grabbing the surf board or kayak and heading into the waves again

Evening:

7) Eat at Voltaco's (Ocean City) or Piatti (La Jolla)…either way fresh tomatoes will be involved!

8) Walk to the boardwalk, play video games (preferably Ms. Pac Man) and eat Kohr's Custard (Ocean City), or stroll along the water after dinner and enjoy the breeze (La Jolla)

9) Go to sleep with the air conditioning on (Ocean City), or with the windows open (La Jolla)

Fall

Location: At home in NYC, preferably on a Saturday

Morning:

1) Wake up and go the farmers market around the corner

2) During the week – speak at a college or a high school

3) Go running in Central Park, or golfing with mom in Montclair, NJ

4) Enjoy a lunch of egg and cheese on a bagel (NYC), or a post-golf lunch on the deck at the golf club

Afternoon:

5) Watch the Yankees in the playoffs against the Red Sox

Evening:

6) Go to my favorite NYC pizza place (Keste or Motorino – see Chapter 4) and enjoy a pizza Margherita with my wife

7) Watch some of my favorite fall shows on TV, or perform stand-up at Comix Comedy Club in NYC

Winter

Location: **In the mountains, like at my in-laws place in the Berkshires (Monterey, MA), or near my cousins in the Rocky Mountains of CO**

Morning:

1) Wake up and help my hosts by doing some chores, like chopping wood or shoveling show

2) Eat a warm breakfast of chocolate chip pancakes and syrup

3) Get my snow gear on and go out skiing or tubing for the day

4) Drink hot chocolate after a few hours on the slopes – can you sense a chocolate theme?

Afternoon:

5) Return home as the sun is setting, dry off, and watch the Steelers in the playoffs against the Colts next to a warm fire

Evening:

6) Enjoy a dinner with friends and family of hearty homemade risotto or gnocchi with a veal ragu, accompanied by a fresh bread

7) Head out for dessert at SoCo Creamery (Berkshires), or some other amazing ice cream place

8) Play Risk or Monopoly back home by the fire, until someone achieves supreme domination (namely me), or watch the latest Netflix rental next to the fireplace

9) Crawl into a cozy, warm bed…exhausted from a good, long day

Spring

Location: At home in NYC, or at my parents' place in Hilton Head Island, SC

Morning:

1) Wake up, do some work on my speaking business, and then sip a homemade smoothie with blueberries, milk, yogurt and bananas.

2) Play softball in Central Park with the Gotham Comedy Club softball team (NYC), or go for a run or bike trip with my wife around the island (NYC or Hilton Head)

Afternoon:

3) Golf with my mom or other family and friends (Montclair, NJ or Hilton Head Island, SC)

4) Go to a Yankees game (NYC), eat sausage and popcorn while the Yankees win

Evening:

5) Make a dinner for my wife – perhaps ribollita or some other Tuscan dish (and actually help my wife clean up the mess)

6) Enjoy the longer hours of sunlight by going out for a bike ride in Central Park with my wife

7) Fall asleep thinking about how great my upcoming summer adventures will be

Exercise: Describe, in writing, your "Best Natural High Day" for each season of the year. If you cannot come up with enough experiences that you know give you a consistent natural high in each season, then get to work finding them! Some people say, "I hate the winter [or summer] around here." However, if they had natural highs in place for each season, they might find within themselves the ability to love life a little more.

Summary

The best natural highs are the ones that you create to fit your life plan. These are often referred to as dreams or goals, but the feelings they impart are truly natural highs. As this chapter discussed, some of these pursuits may require much longer commitments than going for a quick run or eating a great meal. If your natural high involves academic achievement, moving to an exotic land, or reaching some inner peace, it may take time. The natural high you ultimately experience may also feel different from traditional highs. Yet in the end, the time spent will likely be worthwhile.

Meditating appears to be more about calm, focus, and positive feelings than euphoria. For those willing to pursue meditation, you may want to do it following that annual flu shot – your immune system will receive more benefit from the shot than it would normally. The only down side to meditating seems to be trying to find someplace quiet in which to do it. I can tell you from personal experience that closets are not the best smelling places in the world.

Regardless of the natural high you choose, there will always be obstacles to achieving that high. Time, money, and negative people will often be reminders that pursuing something that is great for you might not always be easy. However, when you are doing something positive for yourself, it is always worth the effort. Remembering that will help to keep you going. Good luck as you pursue your natural highs. I would love to hear about them if you get a chance. Just shoot me an e-mail with your story at matt@mattbellace.com.

REFERENCES

CHAPTER ONE: HOW TO GET HIGH NATURALLY

1. Denizet-Lewis, B. (2006, June 25) An Anti-Addiction Pill. *The New York Times.*

2. Alexander, B., Beyerstein, B., Hadaway, P., & Coambs, R. (1981). Effect of early and later colony housing on oral ingestion of morphine in rats. *Pharmacology Biochemistry and Behavior*, 15 (4), 571-576.

3. Gordon, H. (2002). Early environmental stress and biological vulnerability to drug abuse. *Psychoneuroendocrinology*, 27: 115-126.

4. Ompad, D., Ikeda, R., Shah, N., Fuller, C., Bailey, S., Morse, E., Kerndt, P., Maslow, C., Wu, Y., Vlahov, D., Garfein, R., & Strathdee, S. (2005). Childhood sexual abuse and age at initiation of injection drug use. *American Journal of Public Health*, 95(4), 703-709.

5. Pennebaker, J. (1997). Writing about emotional experiences as a therapeutic process. *Psychological Science*, 8: 162-166.

6. Gortner, E., Rude, S., & Pennebaker, J. (2006). Benefits of expressive writing in lowering rumination and depressive symptoms. *Behavior Therapy*, 37: 292-303.

7. Klein, K. (2002). Stress, expressive writing, and working memory. In: S.J. Lepore, & J.M. Smyth (Eds.), *The Writing Cure: How Expressive Writing Promotes Health and Emotional Well-Being* (pp. 135-155). Washington DC: American Psychological Association.

8. Mobbs, D., Greicius, M., Abdel-Azim, E., Menon, V., & Reiss, A. (2003). Humor modulates the mesolimbic reward centers. *Neuron*, 40:1041-1048.

9. Levy, B., & Earleywine, M. (2004). Discriminating reinforcement expectancies for studying from future time perspective in the prediction of drinking problems. *Addicitve Behaviors*, 29, 181-190.

10. Turrisi, R. (1999). Cognitive and attitudinal factors in the analysis of alternatives to binge drinking. *Journal of Applied Social Psychology*, 27(7): 1512-1535.

11. Correia, C., Benson, T., & Carey, K. (2005). Decreased substance use following increased in alternative behaviors: A preliminary investigation. *Addictive Behaviors*, 30(1) 19-27.

12. Murphy, J., Barnett, N., & Colby, S. (2006). Alcohol-related and alcohol-free activity participation and enjoyment among college students: A behavioral theories of choice analysis. *Experimental and Clinical Psychopharmacology*, 14(3) 339-349.

13. DeJong, W., & Langford, L. (2002). A typology for campus-based alcohol prevention: Moving toward environmental strategies. *Journal of Studies on Alcohol*, 14 (Suppl.) 140-147.

14. Geir, T. (1996, January 8). Outlook: Eye on the 90's. *US News and World Report*.

15. Hubel, D & Wiesel, T. (1977). Ferrier lecture: Functional architecture of macaque monkey visual cortex. *Proceedings of the Royal Society of London- B, 198*: 1-59.

16. Hubel, D., Weisel, T., & LeVay, S. (1977). Plasticity of ocular dominance columns in monkey striate cortex. *Philosophical Transactions of the Royal Society London- B: Biological Sciences, 278*: 377-409.

17. Candland, D. (1993). Feral children and clever animals. Oxford University Press.

18. Harlow, H. & Griffin, G. (1965). Induced mental and social deficits in rhesus monkeys. In S.F. Osler and R.E. Cooke (Eds.), *The Biosocial Basis of Mental Retardation.* Baltimore: Johns Hopkins Press.

19. Giedd, J. (2004). Structural magnetic resonance imaging of the adolescent brain. *Annals of the New York Academy of Sciences, 1021,* 77-85.

CHAPTER TWO: LAUGHING

1. Mobbs, D., Greicius, M., Azim, E., Menon, V., & Reiss, A. (2003). Humor modulates the mesolimbic reward regions. *Neuron. 40,* 1041-1048.

2. Drevets, W., Gautier, C., Price, J., Kupfer, D., Kinahan, P., Grace, A., Price, J., & Mathias, C. (2001). Amphetamine-induced dopamine release in human ventral striatum correlates with euphoria. *Biological Psychiatry, 49,* 81-96.

3. Fry, W. (1994). The biology of humor. *Humor: International Journal of Humor Research, 7,* 111-126.

4. Hayashi, T., Tsujii, S., Iburi, T., Tamanaha, T., Yamagami, K., Ishibashi, R., Hori, M., Sakamoto, S., Ishii, H., & Murakami, K. (2007). Laughter up-regulates the gene related to NK cell activity in diabetes. 2007. *Biomedical Research. 28*(6), 281-285.

CHAPTER THREE: RUNNING

1. Boecker, H., Sprenger, T., Henriksen, G., Koppenhoefer, M., Wagner, K., Valet, M., Berthele, A., & Tolle, T. (2008). The Runner's High: Opioidergic mechanisms in the human brain. *Cerebral Cortex.* Advanced Access published February 21, 2008.

2. Brown, R., Abrantes, A., Read, J., Marcus, B., Jakicic, J., Strong, D., Oakley, J., Ramsey, S., Kahler, C., Stuart, G., Dubreil, M., & Gordon, A. (2009). Aerobic exercise for alcohol recovery: Rationale, program description and preliminary findings. *Behavior Modification.* 33(2): 220-249.

3. Scott, P. (2006). Fitness: Bodies in motion clean and sober. *The New York Times.* October 12, 2006.

Chapter Four: Eating

1. Davis, C., Levitan, R., Reid, C., Carter, J., Kaplan, A., Patte, K., King, N., & Kennedy, J. (2009). Dopamine for "wanting" and opioids for "liking": A comparison of obese adults with and without binge eating. *Obesity,* March, 12: E-publication ahead of print, p. 1-6.

2. Hayward, M., & Low, M. (2005). Naloxone's suppression of spontaneous and food-conditioned locomotor activity is diminished in mice lacking either the dopamine D(s) receptor or enkephalin. *Brain Research: Molecular Brain Research, 140*: 91-98.

3. Avena, N., Rada, P., & Hoebel, B. (2009). Sugar and fat bingeing have notable differences in addictive-like behavior. *The Journal of Nutrition,* 139: 623-628.

4. Avena, N., Bocarsly, M., Rada, P., Kim, A. & Hoebel, B. (2008). After daily bingeing on a sucrose solution, food deprivation induces anxiety and accumbens dopamine/acetylcholine imbalance. *Physiology & Behavior, 94*: 309-315.

5. Allen, N., Beral, V., Casabonne, D., Kan, S., Reeves, G., Brown, A., & Green, J. (2009). Moderate alcohol intake and cancer incidence in woman. *Journal of the National Cancer Institute, 101* (5), 296-305.

6. Paul, C., Au, R., Fredman, L., Massaro, J., Seshadri, S., DeCarli, C. & Wolf, P. (2008). Association of alcohol consumption with brain volume in the Framingham study. *Archives of Neurology, 65* (10), 1363-1367.

CHAPTER FIVE: UNHEALTHY NATURAL HIGHS

1. Welte, J., Barnes, G., Tidwell, M., & Hoffman, J. (2008). The prevalence of problem gambling among U.S. adolescents and young adults: Results from a national survey. *Journal of Gambling Studies, 24*, 119-133.

2. Toneatto, T. & Dragonetti, R. (2008). Effectiveness of community-based treatment for problem gambling: A quasi-experimental evaluation of cognitive-behavioral vs. twelve-step therapy. *The American Journal on Addictions, 17*, 298-303.

3. Dodd, M., Klos, K., Bower, J., Geda, Y., Josephs, K., & Ahlskog, E. (2005). Pathological gambling caused by drugs used to treat Parkinson's Disease. *Archives of Neurology, 62*, 1377-1388.

4. Volkow, N., Wang, G., Fowler, & Telang, F. (2008). Overlapping neuronal circuits in addiction and obesity: Evidence of systems pathology. *Philosophical Transactions of the Royal Society of London. Series B, Biological Sciences, 363* (1507), 3191-3200.

5. Torgan, C. (2002). Childhood obesity on the rise. Retrieved October 3, 2009, from http://www.nih.gov/news/WordonHealth/jun2002/childhoodobesity.htm

6. Trasande, L. & Chatterjee, S. (2009). The impact of obesity on health service utilization and costs in childhood. *Obesity*, March 19.

7. Sacks, F., Bray, G., Carey, V., Smith, S., & Ryan, D. (2009). Comparison of weight-loss diets with different compositions of fat, protein, and carbohydrates. *The New England Journal of Medicine, 360*, 859-873.

8. Mond, J., Hay, P., Rodgers, B., & Owen, C. (2006). An update on the definition of "excessive exercise" in eating disorder research. *International Journal of Eating Disorders, 39*, 147-153.

9. Shroff, H., Reba, L., Thornton, L., Tozzi, F., Klump, K., Berrettini W., Brandt H., Crawford S., Crow S., Fichter M., Goldman D., Halmi K., Johnson C., Kaplan A., Keel P., LaVia M., Mitchell J., Rotondo., Strober M., Treasure J., Woodside D., Kaye W., & Bulik C. (2006). Features associated with excessive exercise in women with eating disorders. *International Journal of Eating Disorders. 39* (6), 454-461.

10. Field, A., Cheung, L., Wolf, A., Herzog, D., Gortmaker, S., & Colditz, G. (1999). Exposure to the mass media and weight concern among girls. *Pediatrics, 103*, E53.

11. Caine, D., & Watson, J., (2000). Neuropsychological and neuropathological sequelae of cerebral anoxia: a critical review. *Journal of the International Neuropsychological Society, 6*, 86-99.

12. Hopkins, R., & Haaland, K. (2004). Neuropsychological effects of anoxic or ischemic induced brain injury. *Journal of the International Neuropsychological Society, 10*, 957- 961.

13. Brown, L., Houck, C., Grossman, C., Lescano, C., & Frenkel, J. (2008). Frequency of adolescent self-cutting as a predictor of HIV risk. *Journal of Developmental and Behavioral Pediatrics, 29* (3), 161-165.

14. Suyemoto, K. (1998). The functions of self-mutilation. *Clinical Psychology Review, 18* (5), 531-554.

CHAPTER SIX: HELPING

1. Giving USA (2006). *The Annual Report on Philanthropy for the Year 2006.* Giving Institute.

2. Moll, J., Krueger, F., Zahn, R., Pardini, M., Olivera-Souza, R., & Grafman, J. (2006). Human fronto-mesolimbic networks guide decisions about charitable donation. *Proceedings for the National Academy of Sciences, 103* (42), 15623-15628.

3. Zak, P., Stanton, A., & Ahmadi, S. (2007). Oxytocin increases generosity in humans. *Public Library of Science, One, 2*(11): e1128.

4. Tankersley, D., Stowe C., & Huettel S. (2007). Altruism is associated with an increased neural response to agency. *Nature Neuroscience, 10*(2), 150-151.

CHAPTER SEVEN: LOVING

1. Zeki, S. (2007). The neurobiology of love. *Federation of European Biological Societies. 581*, 2575-2579.

2. O'Connor, M., Wellisch, D., Stanton, A., Eisenberger, N., Irwin, M., & Lieberman, M. (2008). Craving love? Enduring grief activates brain's reward center. *NeuroImage 42* (2): 969-972.

3. Insel, T. (2003). Is social attachment an addictive disorder? *Physiology and Behavior, 79* (3), 351.

CHAPTER EIGHT: CREATING – YOUR OWN NATURAL HIGH

1. Davidson, R., Kabat-Zinn, J., Schumacher, J., Rosenkranz, M., Muller, D., Santorelli, S., Urbanowski, F., Harrington, A., Bonus, K., & Sheridan, J. (2003). Alterations in brain and immune function produced by mindfulness meditation. *Psychosomatic Medicine, 65*, 564-570.

2. Patra, S & Telles, S. (2009). Positive impact of cyclic meditation on subsequent sleep. *Medical Science Monitor, 15*(7), 375-381.

3. Teasdale, J, Williams, J, Soulsby, J, Segal, Z, Ridgeway, V & Lau, M. (2000). Prevention of relapse/recurrence in major depression by mindfulness-based cognitive therapy. *Journal of Consulting and Clinical Psychology, 68*(4), 615-623.

4. Kiecolt-Glaser, J., Glaser, R., Gravenstein, S., Malarkey, W., Sheridan, J. (1996). Chronic stress alters the immune response to influenza virus vaccine in older adults. *Proceedings of the National Academy of Science, USA, 93*, 3043-3047.

5. Davidson, R. (1992). Emotion and affective style: Hemispheric substrates. *Psychological Science, 3*, 39-43.